Rose Hunter is the author of six books of poetry, including *Anchorage* and *glass*. Her poetry has appeared widely in literary journals in Australia, the USA, and Canada, and she has been awarded an Australia Council for the Arts grant. Rose has always drawn on her own experiences in her poetry, but in the last few years she has become interested in writing in a clearer way about her history. She is a survivor of the sex industry and intimate partner violence, and she is an alcoholic and addict in recovery. Born in Armidale, Australia, and raised all over the place, Rose went on to live in Canada for ten years, then Mexico for ten more. She is currently on the Gold Coast, and is enrolled in a PhD in Creative Writing at Griffith University.

Other books by Rose Hunter

Poetry
Anchorage (2020)
glass (2016)
You As Poetry (2013)
[four paths] (2012)
to the river (2010)

Chapbooks
fish and feathers (2017)
descansos (2015)

BODY SHELL GIRL

— *A Memoir* —

Rose Hunter

We respectfully acknowledge the wisdom of Aboriginal
and Torres Strait Islander peoples and their custodianship
of the lands and waterways. Spinifex offices are situated
on Djiru and Bunurong Country.

First published by Spinifex Press, 2022

Spinifex Press Pty Ltd
PO Box 5270, North Geelong, VIC 3215, Australia
PO Box 105, Mission Beach, QLD 4852, Australia

women@spinifexpress.com.au
www.spinifexpress.com.au

Copyright © Rose Hunter, 2022

The moral right of the author has been asserted.

All rights reserved. Without limiting the rights under copyright
reserved above, no part of this publication may be reproduced,
stored in or introduced into a retrieval system, or transmitted,
in any form or by any means (electronic, mechanical, photocopying,
recording or otherwise) without prior written permission of both
the copyright owner and the above publisher of the book.

Copying for educational purposes
Information in this book may be reproduced in whole or part for
study or training purposes, subject to acknowledgement of the source
and providing no commercial usage or sale of material occurs.
Where copies of part or whole of the book are made under part VB
of the Copyright Act, the law requires that prescribed procedures
be followed. For information contact the Copyright Agency Limited.

Edited by Susan Hawthorne and Pauline Hopkins
Cover design by Deb Snibson, MAPG
Typesetting by Helen Christie, Blue Wren Books
Typeset in Albertina
Printed by McPherson's Printing Group

A catalogue record for this book is available from the National Library of Australia

ISBN: 97819259590502 (paperback)
ISBN: 97819259590519 (ebook)

Indeed, the vivid and precise return of the event appears, as modern researchers point out, to be accompanied by an *amnesia* for the past, a fact striking enough to be referred to by several major writers as a *paradox*.

—Cathy Caruth, author *Trauma: Explorations in Memory*

Contents

I.

Portal, 1997	3
Just in the Room	11
Snow Peas	18
This Gets Messed up Pretty Quickly	24
Hungry Ghost Poem	32
In Dreams I Can't Remember, Imagining a Better World	37
Rick	41
Ladybugs and Wishes	45
The Deeper You Go, into the Ocean	48
Chariot	52

II.

Well I Got to Vancouver and All I Found Were Brothels	59
More Than the Strangest Stranger to Me	64
Rent Day	65
Red Velvet Suite	68
An Act of Glossing Over	79
Circus Poem	81
Head Shelves and Crawlspaces	82
Gravel	84

III.

Home Sweet	101
On Jarvis	108
Why We Are Girls	111
Mr Donut	113
I Am	116
He Is	118
Aquarium	121
Money: Some (More) Points	126
In Dreams and in the Dead	129
Future Poem	132
Epilogue	139
Notes	143
Acknowledgements	147

I

Portal, 1997

i

Look, for months I ignored those ads
you know the ones, maybe:

Masseuses wanted!
$$$
cash paid DAILY
no experience necessary
!!!

Classified section of the *Toronto Star* cast out over
peanut butter brown, hardwood floors
of that share apartment near St Clair and Bathurst
black ink on fingertips, red pen poised:
retail, waitressing, shelf stocking
I got some interviews
I got a job in a photo shop

lasted three weeks before I went to lunch
permanently, seriously
required to sit staring into space
when there was nothing to do
which was often
my 'storybooks' as the manager called them, banned

it wasn't the first time I'd come across that
and been amazed
the others could do it!
How

I tried and went crazy

so back to the start, I got an interview
a paid internship at a documentary film company
a dream job. Hanging everything on getting that job

which was a sure way for the universe not
to give it to you
not that I believed in that sort of thinking
but really I did, and really I didn't
yet I was flying high
with imagining it, dizzy with wanting
and wishing and waiting
for my housemate's phone to ring

but then it did
and it was no

the room echoed, the finality snapping
shut
but snap out of it, I'd try again

but for now I needed a job, any job
I got more interviews
but didn't get those jobs either

demoralising, like my job searches always were
turns out a BA in English didn't qualify me for much
and crumbling: the dream-wish that somehow
during this year's working visa in Canada

I'd get that job I never could get in Australia
I'd keep that job I never could keep there
I'd find that home I never could there
and my life would finally start
but instead

rent loomed

and nothing in reserve
to qualify for the visa I'd borrowed money
got a printout of that bank statement
as my 'proof of sufficient funds'
then gave the money back
I considered it a victimless crime

but oh no, what to do now
and so, one day
a neat steady circle

appeared around one of those ads
it was my hand that held the pen
I watched it join the curved edges of the line
then pause
a tiny red moon formed
which I smudged into a red comet

I stared at it. Picked up the phone.
Pressed two spirals of the cord
between my thumb and forefinger
allowed them to ease apart
pressed them together again
put the phone back. Ate a packet of Doritos
calculated this would take me approx.
half an hour to run off
kneeled in front of the toilet bowl
but no no, not now, do not

even let that idea in
God no no
I'd never call if I started on that
I picked up the phone again
my breath like skipping stones

maybe I could get in trouble for even calling?
No experience necessary to be a masseuse?
Well, it didn't say massage therapist.
I'd heard about what they called 'sex work'
in university, and how it was a job like any other
they said. Also a bit radical
and daring and even cool
at least in the groups I tried to fit in with
although none of us actually did it, that I knew of

but I also thought it was mostly illegal
so I didn't think this could be that
if it was advertised in the main newspaper?

Maybe it was something borderline
like lingerie massaging? Did that exist?
Maybe I could do that? Maybe
you know, if I owned lingerie
and if anyone would pay to see me in it
when they saw me they'd laugh me out of the room

probably it was for models
but who knew who it was for
this was back in the days before I owned a computer
and before people googled everything, and life
in many ways, held more surprises

maybe it would be something I could do
it wouldn't mean anything serious to me
like it might for normal people.

"Hello ugh. I'm calling about the ad yes ugh—"
  something like that.
"I love your accent!" The voice on the other end
  like campfires and marshmallows and you're invited

well this was the warmest reaction I'd received
since I arrived in the country; OK maybe not quite
but it was the warmest reaction from anyone
I'd rung about a *job*
so I wrote down the address

an hour and a half later I stepped off the bus
way over on Steeles West
just when you thought there could be no city left
it kept on unfolding
an infinite white and brown chequerboard
the wind hurtled snow across the expanse
of the strip mall parking lot

flying white sparks that pin-pelted my calves
and the patch of ice that crumpled
a numbing, gloving of foot; I was

head down and heading
for the window with red neon
two rectangles outlined in more red neon, polka dots:

MASSAGE
OPEN

a red shadow thrown over Venetian blinds
one side scrunched, the other cycloning out
the tangled string with the loop at the end
a lifebuoy
mine? Or could be, or
call it off
then again nothing ventured
or go back to the bus stop

or deep breath and pull on that door handle

ii.

And what I imagined this place might be:

hazier, shrouded, and looking over shoulders
not crisp plastic maidenhair fern
and reception area like doctor-lawyer-dentist
except with cigarette smoke and hip hop
and platinum blonde, movie star woman
in three-quarter length, I thought blue suede

even if it wasn't, and even if I didn't know really
what blue suede was, really
except for the blue and the soft; a serenade

with envelope collar, four-dice buttons and fitted waist
and welcoming voice from the phone
greeting me as though I was everything she'd been
expecting (huh?); well I followed

her sparkling trail of precious metal glimmering
bracelets clinking and cinnamon wafts, and talk
of wow $$$
and what you had to do:

"Nude hand jobs basically," she said, and shrugged
as though summarising the weather
I met her eyes and nodded, as if to say ah, as I
expected, while my stomach belly-
flopped; how

could you do that
and to any random dude who wandered in? The idea
twisted my flopped stomach
wrung it out like laundry, how gross
and embarrassing; how

did those words flow out of her mouth, like nothing?
I'd never even done a hand job before
not in the beginning-to-end sense
not that I'd admit that to her or anyone
my freakish inexperience
for the ripe old age of twenty-five

but even if I knew how, how could you do that
and the naked part too
the lingerie massaging idea was not naked
big difference; clearly I couldn't do any of this

so why was this Blue Suede
gazing at me with her disco and glitter-lidded eyes
as though seriously entertaining me for this role?

I'd have to meet the boss, she told me
to be hired for real—she'd be here at the shift change
"But in the meantime we need someone, you can
start."
Like when, like right

now? Like
now now?

Maybe I should consider it. It was one man at a time
at least. I'd seen the ads for stripping too
I had not yet put a red circle around one of them.
All those eyes!
There was no way

but just one set of them, that was just one more
than zero, you could see it that way; also

with one man you'd know where he was looking
(this seemed important)
no stage fright and no dancing
and no one else but you and he to witness it
low light and a wig maybe
you could do it like incognito almost
OK but could I

do it? What if I did it wrong, or froze
or turned vermillion, or hyperventilated, or cried
or ran out of the room, or all of the above

well and what if? Humiliation
in front of one man I'd never see again
and back where I am right now. What would I lose?
Here's what I might gain:

$500 to $800 a night!
OK so she was talking about what she was making
and I was no Blue Suede

so subtract a third, or a half
to take that into account (might it work this way?)
still more than enough

for rent, food, transport, boots that didn't leak
a warm coat, and job interview clothes
maybe even like that. Maybe I'd have that internship
if I dressed better? Maybe I'd be someone else
if I dressed better ... Look
wasn't like I was gonna do it for a decade or anything.

Blue suede

with darker blue lining, like deeper
deeper, I caught the glimpse of sapphire
my blue yellow brick road

Just in the Room

i.

A narrow shelf on the right? Rough sawn and splintery
caramel with decorative candle, with
scalloped leaves of holly? Well, it was close to Christmas
but was that this room, close to this Christmas
or some other? Memory, after all, is a shapeshifter
a memory of a memory of a memory of a—could be

a shelf from any of the parlours I was in later
or lassoed in from some other place
to fill those gaps the mind doesn't like
in any case, rough sawn or pearly smooth
holly or some other

a man arrives

and the feeling I had was deciding

he looked a bit like my father
even though my father was hazel-eyed not blue
and not then white-haired
and there were no physical similarities actually
other than *older*
thought: I am manufacturing this
to make myself feel bad

because what I was feeling was a full sort of nothing
replete with the other static:
the hum of the yellow lights
the soft swishing of the snow-faring traffic on Steeles
and then I was just in the room
and out of it

and floating in between

and he was on the table
holding up his hands like stop
when I went for the light

"I want to see you."
Which gave me the flash of an impression that this was

really happening, and I was
really there

whereas before I thought maybe watching at the keyhole
another clueless young woman in shapeless skirt
and faded black tee (because black was slimming, right
except this was more like slate grey, anyway)
or had run away

a child tumbling
through the chequerboard tundra; forgot

to use the fake name, considered that a faux pas
or bad omen, or immediate screw-up
then again that must be more important if you're from here
I mean if you knew people here
that you didn't want finding out

although how would a fake name help that? I wondered
unless you had an unusual real name
hmm so maybe just a way to remind yourself
you're an *actress*
like Blue Suede had said

another bad omen: I was no good at acting
I thought. I didn't yet know I had some relevant talents
for example the ability to keep what I was thinking hidden
it was usually wrong
therefore pause, observe

what other people did and said
I had that mind waiting in the wings like that
near the hinge
nestled against the shoulder muscle, crouched

and in the meantime smile and nod, or laugh
(where a laugh was a twitch toward
the idea of a laugh
then stopped); also knew

how running the mind was a way for the body to stay still
(stay in the room)
and that I

was worth something in those instances in which
I pleased others. A pant leg with sock streamer

and bills, partially folded, lengthwise
open palms
the green grass green of three Canadian twenties
and I remembered what Blue Suede said
I was supposed to do for that
still I pulled my T-shirt a hand's length away from my body
and tilted my head at him, in case I had it wrong

"Yes *please*," he said, smiling as though anticipating
a delicious dinner; huh, really
huh, and how

I was right now tumbling
through that chequerboard tundra
or on a bus on Steeles
screaming at myself (in my head)
for being such a coward
for *running*

back to square one
and square two: eviction or
that plane ticket, back to where I'd come from

and never wanted to be, and missed opportunity
in this grand city, chock-filled with them
(I knew I'd be OK here like I wasn't there)
the fresh start and how everything would be different
in my life from now on, if only I could stay

a cold lake came to mind and how the way was to jump
casting off all objections

as he turned, bit more
bit more, the side of his chin on his upturned hand
his gelled hair-crown, pavlova like
white belly tumbling to rest on the table
other hand on his hip; a misplaced blasé

comedy odalisque? Or a fleshy sconce? Ruddy nose
and sweating eyes, lazy smile
flickering in the yellow light
I lifted my shirt over my head and stepped out of my skirt
like I was in the room alone
or like I knew there was someone at the keyhole but
ignoring that, or like an apology

not sure

my big toe hooked on my underwear coming off, half
tripped, then gazing around; where to put them
my cheeks a rising warmth
his face a clearing house of amaze

seashells rattle-pulled with the retreat of a wave
eyes adjusting, his jaw actually (literally)
dropping

"I really am your first!"

And I didn't understand why it was, but understood
that it was

"*So good.*"

ii.

Not good
no time
to think
just grab
the oil bottle
the dark curly hairs around the rim
that made me almost retch

then turn my back to wipe them away
with a Kleenex, before he saw

and as though this
was the most mortifying thing here

"Pour the oil into your hands first," he said.
"Rub them together, warm it, that's right,"

his hand reaching over to cover mine
the wrinkles around his eyes, deepening
and big phew!
That he was old, I thought

it made it less real

on the table like a floppy white seal
ghostly and strange
and guiding my hand
to this gelatinous part of him
like a small pink sea cucumber

how strange how strange how strange

and how if I kept repeating that
I couldn't hear my other thoughts
and so I kept repeating it
how strange how strange how strange
gelatinous in my hand

as he squirmed and writhed
grappling sweaty
hand clamped onto my boob, what
I jumped

then blushed
embarrassed by my incorrect reaction
I thought, or the fact that he was
a complete stranger

who does this? Then giggled
to cover all that

he gasped
as though I'd done something to hurt him?
Fumbled at my other boob
reaching from one to the other
sloppy, flipper like
or a series of frenzied last-minute

panic attacks? Oh no
was he having a fit

or a heart attack? Like I'd seen happen
to old men with young women
like in movies, oh God oh God

should I call 000
or what was it in Canada
same as the US, 911 right?
Yell for help first, or what

I sweated, frozen and wide-eyed
(in my head)
but pretended like casual
in case this was normal
as I waited for more information

a surge of almost firmness in my hand
then gone
his scrunched-up face, whimpering
relaxing, sighing

between my fingers
white stretching sticky
like that Clag Paste I remembered
from what, primary school?
The triangular container with the red label
and lid with little brush

how strange how strange how strange

it was to be thinking about that now
and now what

now what now what?

"You're a natural," he said.
Well, I

had never been called that before
with respect to anything.

Snow Peas

"You are what they call *rough around edges*."

This was the boss, Zuzanna
nose pinched to a peak and cheeks smooth as teacups
and rumbling underwater deliciousness
of her Eastern European accent

a glance from the top of my frizzy hair to my bare feet
frowning and sighing, was it
despair? Look what turned up in the latest snowstorm

well, I cringed and aimed my gaze at the fern
I knew she was about to tell me I was too
rough around edges
to take my $140, and leave

$140!

An unreal amount for me to now have
tucked in the side pocket of my beat-up handbag
mere hours after the only thing there had been five bucks
some chewing gum, and a strip of perforated bus tickets

$140: two times the $60 extra, or tip, as they also called it
for the two nude-with-touching 'massages'
(neither of them had involved much actual massaging)
plus $10 out of each of the two $40 session fees
I kept slipping my hand into that side pocket
to check the bills were still there

and now, I couldn't believe I'd been given this
glimpse of a solution to all my problems
only to have it ripped away

"Rough around edges, *boyo*." Zuzanna said, nodding at me
like I was a street dog maybe
found rooting through the garbage, a mottled mess of mange?
"But."

But? There was a but? I glanced up, eyes lit
up

"But

talk funny and look like the schoolteacher, so no worry.
Some men they like this. You take money from today
get make-up and dress for tomorrow night."

Tomorrow night?
Did that mean?

In my mind I leapt up and hugged her. In reality
I beamed and nodded, in quick shallow successions
yes yes yes!

"And clean up eyebrows, for the love of Mary
this is forest you have." She leaned in close to my face
shaking her head, then stepped back and waved her hand
wand like and looping squiggles: "I don't know what this is
and other parts I can't see, I just guess."

My face burned, and I stared into my hands
but OK OK so what, the point was I could
stay?

"Call me Zu," my new boss said
and I marvelled at that word, 'boss'
how it made it seem like this was normal
that 'job like any other' that people talked about; so OK

as Zu pulled Styrofoam containers out of plastic bags
lined them up on the coffee table like white stepping stones
spooned some from each onto a paper plate

its bulging middle and spreading warmth
snow peas glistening on steaming white rice
with clicking plastic knives and forks
and I wondered how I'd landed here

more than I'd wondered it in the room
the room being a sort of event
that may or may not have happened, or
to be processed later
bulky, but possible to ignore
like sitting amongst all this packaging or really unimportant
elephant relatives in the room, and
"Boyo," (as Zu might say)

in a city in which I knew nothing and no one
some kind of miracle it seemed to me
to be in this cosy, backroom office

with Blue Suede too, whose name was Lisa
telling a story about a 'client', as they called them
(so polite too, like doctor-lawyer-dentist)

and Zu's husband, Tomasz
his round face like a large pale bear
hunched over his plate
his twitching shoulders and half smile, there but not
exactly, or heard it all before, maybe

while Zu doubled over, a torrent-shriek, then straightened
gazing up, up, as she dragged a tissue rolled into a point
along the bottom of her eye
as though the trace of a tear on skin must be staunched
as though water and salt were beginnings of ruins
this image of femininity
its sharp tools and bodily refusals

so strange, yet I thought I would try to become it
(at least a bit)
I thought it might give me value

OK, but the story
was gross and not even believable?
Who would do that? *Next* to the toilet? And leave it there?
But seeing they didn't question it
and so laughing along too.
"I can tell," Zu said, turning to me, "That you're a nice girl
a good girl. So I give you advice. Don't
turn into one of those other girls,"

she held her forefinger up
the three folded fingers in front
terraces with talons, glinting like brake lights: "Don't

start with the partying and the booze and the drugs
and the bad boyfriends who take your money
don't give your money to no man."
I shook my head, of course not
who would?
"And don't do full service. Ever. Don't even think about it."

Well, I gazed at her, waiting for further information
she gazed back
her mouth flew open
her fingernails biffed the top of my head
but gently, like a caress.
"Sex!" she shrieked. "Don't do sex!"

"Oh." I felt the slow hot creeping over my cheeks again
God, why would she think I would
and what a bizarre term for it that was
as though men might break down
like cars by the side of the road?

"I don't care how hot he is," Zu said.
"And not just because of shit pile you get me into
the cops they leave us alone if we don't do that
but I want you to remember this: you are not a whore."
Her grey-green eyes fixed on me; well

I didn't get the distinction between hand jobs
and this 'full service' on a morality level
but whoa obviously big difference on a bodily level.
"I am never doing full service, don't worry."
I felt my head draw back into my chin and mouth crinkle up
triple ew, and no way—

"Ah!" Zu clapped her hands. "You are the lesbian?
I thought so. Perfect for this. Perfect!"
I hesitated at her beaming face
I wasn't about to tell her I didn't think anyone was hot
if 'hot' meant 'made me want to have sex with them'
or that I was equally nonplussed by everyone's naked body

I knew my feelings were wrong wrong
as well as the direct opposite of cool
everyone said so, as well as TV, films, advertising, etc.,
although it was also true that I hadn't
seen many naked people

maybe this strange gig would cure me?
Maybe all I needed was to see more of them
then I'd be as fascinated with them as other people were
clearly there was something so wrong wrong
with me that I wasn't

"You can keep your eyes on your goals," Zu said.
"Like Lisa. She's doing a degree."
"Final year," Lisa said, sifting round in her rice. Well, now
my ears pricked up like frost tipped
and the whole world sparked with

possibility. Maybe this could pay for more than rent.
Like qualifications for a job I actually wanted
like that internship
a career I wanted, even

maybe I could go to film school!
They were crazy expensive
but if I could make that kind of money? Film school ...

"My best girl." Zu beamed at Lisa like a proud parent.
"I lose her soon. But better this way.
I sleep good this way.
You're lucky you're in here with us, Rose.
The others, they won't tell you this.
But you're lucky, and now you can be smart too." Well
I was not used to being *in*

anywhere, *with* anyone. Then they gave me a lift
all the way home! Snow peas like little green teeth
green bubble wrap green banners green messages of green

This Gets Messed up Pretty Quickly

i.

In russet brown with sparkles like twinkle twinkle
plunging neckline and a feel of suede
bought from the Bay (classy!) and paid for with cash
(maybe not classy)
I waited for the clerk to give me a glance, like
where was someone like me
gonna wear a dress like this?
She didn't even look up

but Zu did: mouth turned down like a setting sun
eyebrow slivers raised
(mine, freshly attacked with tweezers
uneven; oh dear)—but Zu
nodding into her chin
and I glowed

as Lisa gave me the thumbs up
she and Phoenix, couch dancing to Biggie
to Puff Daddy, to Shania; the click of Deja's
clear heels on tile and shale-like layered
haze of the smoky room
in which I was sitting, book out: Atwood, Gowdy,
Munro, a Jim Jarmusch film script ... between
rumble tumble BZZZT!—of the dryer, and talk

of money dresses, money nights
and money rooms, what was that
some more pleasing size or shape or arrangement of
massage table and chair?

And money hustles
I called them scripts, or spiels
pick one and use it every time, they said

it saved thinking
still, that mind bump
sometimes a mind mountain
over which I'd ask myself the questions,

"Do you want to stay here or not?" (Where *there*
wasn't just a geographical place
but a history to be forgotten)
and, "Do you want to go to film school or not?"
This got me back on track
I mean wait
to see if he'd ask for extras

but not too long
even though it was the soliciting that was illegal
as I understood it (which was not well)
the saying anything about it
but saying nothing, sometimes
"Jizz all over your hands for ten bucks,"
as Phoenix put it

OK so deep breath
think of that lake (jump

in); what kind of answers
are offered in a box-like room? What kind of chair

is in the corner (colour, style, dimensions, please)
I don't know why
I search for details like these
or why it's my wish rocket
to go back and *know*: what kind of ceiling?
Speckled egg or solid
matte, popcorn, or buff

no, I can't see that, but I can see me
in bird's-eye view
a barn swallow's say, mud nest flush with ceiling
hair, feathers, grasses, moss, peeling

a memory of an image I never saw:
a blank-faced brunette (before the dye job)
staring up, up
for answers or to pass the time

ii.

So the 'nude reverse' as they called it, the $60 tip
the 'reverse' part of it supposed to mean
the man (all the customers were men)
could give you a massage as well, or a 'massage'
on your boobs and ass cheeks only, Lisa reassured me
"Don't let their skanky paws go anywhere else,"
and some of them did give me an actual massage
like on the back or the feet, etc.,
but other times here's how that went:

moving my ass back, back
as his hand moved forward, forward
crotch height and incoming
until I'd be bent over with arms reaching out
(to do the massage)
while ass attempting to point skyward
while he'd be half falling off the table, arm-eel flail

"No no no," equals, "Blah blah blah,"

really?
I couldn't understand it, I mean weren't they ashamed
to keep trying when I kept saying no no no?

But what I quickly understood: in most cases
keep moving away, keep moving away
you could make it all the way
to 'time's up' this way

take your money and leave

iii.

So the 'body slide' as they called it, the $80–$100 tip:
dump that oil in your palm
smear it on your boobs
knees between his legs
hands gripping the towel-covered table further up
ass up and slither (a weird thing to do, I thought

I mean, why?). First time like seriously
where does this hand go
and how not to fall on top of him
or crash off the table, and why was someone
with my coordination skills even doing this?
But after a few times it was OK

and the cold sweating was OK too
plus in this position they couldn't get at your crotch
for that reason, as well as the money
after a while if a guy was a newbie or from out of town
it was the only extra I'd mention:
"A fun massage or a boring massage?"

that was Lisa's line I copied
and even though body slides were not
strictly speaking allowed
"Too easy it leads to something else," Zu said
but "Ignore that," Lisa said,
"If you're here to make money
just don't let it lead to something else."
And I nodded, no problem there

one time a guy came in
razor-ad face and flexing-his-muscles walk
Tanya and Deja in my ear gushing
how lucky I was he picked me, because he was so *hot*

OK, so I could definitely appreciate
aesthetically pleasing people

especially faces; however
this did not make me want to see those people naked
or touch their genitals
but I nodded along, to fit in

"You girls are in la-la land," Phoenix said,
   zipping up her usual, black leather minidress.
"Does he have money? That's all that counts."

What a relief, I thought. That's what I'd say next time
I mean if that conversation happened again.

iv.

So one time this guy, haggling over prices
and pestering about that full service
"We don't do that here," I told him
   but copying how I'd heard the other girls say it
soothing-chirpy plus second person plural
not a personal rejection
just something *we* don't do here
for anyone, so sorry.
"Yes you do," he said, and yanked on my boobs
like trying to rip them off a clothesline; where

did they get this stuff from? Porn?
Did they do this to their wives and girlfriends?
So many of them mentioned them
or had wedding rings
if they did this to their wives and girlfriends
what did these women say about it?
Did anyone want this type of mauling?
I didn't know (any of it)

"No no no,"
I kept moving away
he kept moving toward

and sitting up when I tried to massage his feet
and for sure this guy had more than two hands
fully fending off a swarm
but like the girls said:
"Get him off and get him out,"
and since I'd given him a discount
I thought an early finish would be OK; OK

no. Gawwwwwdddd. Right before closing
four a.m. and feet aching
floating with exhaustion and body groped-out

I just wanted to get out of there
I just wanted those swarm hands off me
I just wanted to stop saying, "No no no,"
and seeing how it had no effect

but surely it was almost over
if I hung on a few more minutes
whereas if I left now it might cause an argument
I'd seen it happen to Deja
the guy wanted his whole tip back
because she shorted him like eight minutes
Deja refused, but the guy
yelling in the hall

I didn't want that to happen to me
if it did, likely I'd give him the whole tip back
so he'd stop yelling, and end the embarrassment
my embarrassment, I assumed
for not handling him better
or was it my embarrassment on his behalf

maybe both
anyway, a few more minutes of this
and all that could be avoided

wet sand Brillo-pad hair in pieces and prisms
of amber and old straw, grit
between my fingers
in my palm, the coursing, beginning
and how he'd pull my hand off again (again)

like the shattering of a hope
that smelled like a kick to the throat
in a mouldy cellar
backed up with standing water

no shower in that parlour to ask him to take
which I was even glad of, because
there was another difficult conversation
shame, shame
(mine); for sure someone like Deja
would have *shut this shit down*
whereas I inhaled

head to the side like a swimmer, LOL
OMG like not funny
haha or peculiar, like make it into a song
sing it, "Hahahaaaaa or peculiarrrrrrrrr …"

"I'm a law enforcement officer by the way,"
he said, as he pulled on his pants
belt buckle clicking and badge
like a flash of fender, or like sure
we could talk about the Leafs, but 'eh
in the meantime throw that bit of info

out

my heart dragged into my stomach
my breath
stopped
montage of handcuffs and cell bars and worse:

the whole place going down because of me
because I hadn't asked him who he was
like Lisa told me
but Phoenix said it was garbage; that is
if you asked if he was an 'officer of the law'
(in those words exactly)
if he was, he couldn't say no
I asked it for a while then stopped

because it freaked the men out
who weren't officers of the law
or it made them think I was one
none of which was conducive
to the smooth negotiating of tips—
and now, my fault!

The fear of arrest vs
the fear of having been the dumbshit
who got everyone else arrested *as well*

one or both, was too large to compute

spot-rooted in hot-frozen nowhere land
as he drew the moment out
out

in that small room across
chasms of power
with invisible string
pull
pulling
…

then flashing a grin:
"Don't worry
I'm not on duty."

Hungry Ghost Poem

So the two-litre tub of ice cream and family-sized
block of chocolate, the biggest bag of Cheezies
no, Doritos; no, Cheezies—or should I get cheesecake
Sara Lee, but Cheezies are cheaper
so OK, I headed for the register

then back to the aisles, because shampoo, add that
so the cashier didn't think I was here solely
for that pile of junk food, plus
I did need shampoo; OK, and maybe I'd
throw in a casual comment about a video night
you know, like with that family
advertised on the chocolate

or not, might botch the delivery, make things worse
and most people would assume that sort of thing
because no one would guess what I was really doing
because no one else did this
or, if some people did, they didn't do it as bad as I did
it wouldn't even occur to them
no one was as bad and stupid as this, just me; OK

those three things then, would be enough
maybe too much
I often took the rest to the garbage
when I couldn't cram in one more bite
then I'd cram in one more bite
and another and another, on the way there

this was the garbage in the park across the street
didn't want my housemate to think, hmm
lotta garbage all of a sudden
what *is* all that?
And then I'd have to invent friends

who'd been here and eaten that
big junkfood-eating friends
who also threw the rest out?
No, it was impossible; OK

so those three things would be enough, I mean
it was never enough, but that was a different issue

enough so I wouldn't have to go out again, I meant
for more, mid-binge
my bloated and aching belly
skin raw like sandpaper and flint
throat like after a screaming
primal, from the guttural

and worse, the knowledge of how bad and disgusting
and fat and ugly and stupid and wasteful and worthless

I was
how I did not deserve to live

waiting in line feeling like that
(staring at the ground
praying no one would look at me)
so I could get the more I had to have

to finish the binge
this was the worst of the worst; worse

than kneeling in front of the toilet bowl
middle finger plumbing for the springy softness
just past the back of my tongue
willing the twitch in my stomach to flick over
into the teeth-grabbing heaving
the warm mouth-filling gushing
but more often: the retching choppy
scattering of shreds and shards

a lousy puker, another thing I was useless at
if I could do that right I wouldn't be fat
loser, loser, and worse

than pulling on my sneakers
dragging my lug-heavy body through the mud slush
or following the herringbone and heel-divoted
half-moons in the snow, under the blue sky
shuffle running with legs like stones
and stomach like a bucket of water
hauling in air
and dream-wishing

I just hadn't eaten any of that
if only I just hadn't

because afterwards it always seemed possible
not to have done it
so stupid, stupid; how
could I have done it, again?
If only I hadn't
everything would be OK right now
and I had said that hundreds of times

I was *disgraceful*
ugly, a monster, and my other childhood name:
the *Stupid Thing*

Exhibit A, proving it true
that I was that same six-year-old who ate until it hurt
and wanted more, and that same eight-year-old
who discovered those names could slide right off
with an ease directly dependent
on the quantity of food sliding down my throat

they could not touch me here; that I was that same
ten- and twelve-year-old who dreamed
of a life in which there was nothing else to do but eat
if there was a way the food could

drain out? As soon as I stuffed it in?
And my stomach would never hurt
eating alone in a sealed room without pause and forever
my idea of heaven; that I was that same

teenager on diet after diet
so hungry always, so empty
and here I was again, the diet I was on this time
to lose weight for the parlour

Zu had taken me on in spite of my extra kilos
but I knew if I lost weight more men would pick me
and I'd make more money
and I'd feel better about them seeing me naked
and Zu would approve
and if I was thin everyone would like me
at the parlour and everywhere else; why

was this cashier taking so long?
Was it for me, so I could change my mind
put the ice cream back
but five people behind me
if I left now I'd have to wait longer when I returned
which would be straight away, almost
these last-minute attempts to resist never worked
this I knew:

the binge was its own jangled beast
it started when it said it started
it finished when it said it finished.

My mouth paste and falling water, and emptiness
stretched
my body, a hole that hurt
like arms and legs and bones were empty stomachs too
screaming to be filled

go on, open the chocolate now
everyone would see
but could I make a joke about no lunch? God, what
arguing over a coupon, and worse

I couldn't go to the parlour tonight after this.
I'd gone there once after a binge
it was the pits
those hands all over
bloated sandpaper detested body

like bull ants hoarding over
a stumped open wound
when all I wanted was to curl up in bed
wish myself dead

stupid stupid
and when I was saving for film school too

I'd call and tell Zu I couldn't come in
she wouldn't mind
girls were no-shows all the time
that was one advantage of this gig
a big advantage for me, considering
OK so what this was then: one last blowout

before the diet that was restarting right after
and that was going to work, this time. This time
would be different, and no, I didn't think what
would be different this time so as to

make it different; this time would be different because
it just *would*
because it had to be, because who
would ever, do this again

no one would

no one would

In Dreams I Can't Remember, Imagining a Better World

How I told my housemate I got a job at a Coffee Time
graveyard shift, way out on Steeles
(so she wouldn't decide to drop in)
"Nice coat," she said, and yikes

I thought, should've said bartending at least
if I bought anything else like that (my new white coat!
Toasty warm dream with fleecy hood, with faux fur trim)—
I'd say I'd quit Coffee Time, now bartending
or cocktail waitressing
or rich boyfriend? I didn't know anything
about bartending or cocktail waitressing or rich boyfriends
(or working at a Coffee Time)

but I was getting used to the lies
Lisa told her boyfriend the place was a spa
(which was what parlours were sometimes called too)
only a legit one, of course
and she was a part-time beautician; "Use that," she said.
But the last thing I looked like was a beautician, I thought
keep it in the realm of the credible
and Andrea and Tanya told some friends
they worked at a massage parlour, but as receptionists

there were no receptionists at that parlour
whoever was near the phone answered it
and we took turns going to the door
but other people didn't know that, I guessed
still, it seemed flimsy to me
Deja told her friends she was a drug dealer
"It explains the cash," she said. "And the hours,"

but I knew I didn't have the streetwise vibe
to claim that clearly more respectable gig
and how I was thinking about all that

so that I felt that elbow
in the way that you feel an insect

buzzing around your ear
shoo it away while you keep on talking
or put the butter back in the refrigerator; also
eyeing the people in seats, waiting

for someone to close a magazine or zip up a bag—
which row would be best to go stand next to
pressing into a sliver between the other standing people
so it expanded, enough to slip through. But again
that elbow, jolting as the bus jolted, I thought

only this was the small of my back
so, weird elbow …?

I stepped into the stair gutter and swung around
in front of me: sweatpants, fleecy with pilling fabric
and yep, weird elbow

I reached for the bellpull
the door pleated open
the ground ran like grain
as I waited

for the bus to come to a complete
stop.

Then stepped off, smooth
as though eyes were on me and it was my job to act
as though nothing out of the ordinary had just happened
(huh?). My legs hollow and heavy and light
and then there was the snowstorm
and it had not been my stop! What

and why hadn't I realised earlier? No one
on the bus had seen? Surely if they had
they would have said something. What if they saw
and thought I knew about it? Or they thought I was into it?
Because otherwise they would have said something

right? Sweat prickled my back
and I squirmed in my coat, now white outer husk
of my confusion
I mean at least at the parlour you signed up for it
but on the bus

on the way there?

My face burned at how I'd fled
for sure Phoenix would have punched him in the balls
and Lisa would have announced to everyone on the bus
what he'd been doing (really? No one had seen?)
and Deja would have laughed in his face

why hadn't I?
With the icy wind burning my cheeks into brittle
I thought of that doctor with his unexpected
'breast examination', and the landlord with the porno
and the other landlord who'd appeared at the door, dick out
and so many other non-parlour *incidents*

as I called them, filed away as one-offs
strange occurrences
(one one-off strange occurrence after another)

as well as how I'd slunk away, in snowstorms
or like on creaky floorboards that might give way

well, later I decided to disown all that.

Pretend it had never been mine.
So this was the water I was swimming in anyway, I said
(to myself)
but blasé like now, as though I had always known
hell

in that case may as well get paid

Rick

How he put one thumb on top of the other
then switched it with the other (and again)
thumb patting and mumbling into his blushing neck
as he called me 'beautiful'; a 'knockout'?
Had to stop myself from scratching my head
or glancing behind me, huh? Or, some days

maybe it was true? Peeking in the mirror
and sucking in my stomach
or maybe I had always been too hard on my looks
or was it just at this angle or in this light
my ego ricocheted around like a pool hall break

as, "There's the budding filmmaker," he'd say
because I'd told him about my plans
I pictured myself at the school already
the snow-capped mountains in the distance
the soundtrack surging, inspirational
along with glossy images:
twentysomethings in skater gear and band T-shirts
in front of green screens, holding light meters
bent over viewfinders or boom poles
or deep in discussion … And Rick

he even went to see *Cube* and *The Sweet Hereafter*
instead of *Titanic*
because I told him to, and he always asked
before touching me, then asked again, if it was OK
hands like feathers
that felt like tarantulas
or tonnes; time

    stre..tched

how the assholes were easier, mostly
than the ones I liked
enough to wish this was not how I knew them
but deep breath

think of the vodka I'd swigged in the toilet stall
(extra swigs because it was Rick)
wait for that to kick
in

think of my body as a shell
that I could vacate, not as metaphor, or symbol
but as a real possibility

and when I slid my hand up from his thigh
(that lake again; good; leap

in)
he pressed his shoulders into the table
puffed his chest out and hummed, a single tone
a high-pitched beep test
and added a shoulder dance
so dorky
also the kind of thing I could see myself doing
a moment to try to imagine that

being him
wanting this
?

And he'd say things like
"I'd tell you you don't have to do that part
but I can't, I'm sorry, I love that part,"
and chuckle, his voice catching in his throat
one time he coughed so much
had to go out and get him a glass of water
sit there patting him on the back

"Don't be sorry," I said. "I love to do it for you."
(The key to saying this convincingly was no hesitation
no leap in this case; already in.)
"Really?" He fixed his gaze on me
as though waiting for an

honest answer?
"Really." And I watched the furrows in his brow relax
like a rug shaken
on a sunny day with bluebells and squishy toys

guilt over my lie twinged me
even though I knew an honest reply
would have meant never seeing him again
and losing a good regular
('good' meaning good tip, as well as a half hour
in which you knew what you were dealing with)

and then there was relief
that he didn't ask for details

like tell me why you love it, like many of them did
at which point my mind would go blank
the porn-talk script I'd tried to memorise
(cobbled together from what I heard other girls say)
gone—
and I had zero talent for improvisation
and with the men who kept insisting
I was then blank and blanker

and felt like crying
at a loss as to why I couldn't blather something out
in my later years I was to joke about it
why I could do the job, but not talk about it
in the ways they wanted me to talk about it

"I care about *words*," I'd say
(to myself mostly, but also once or twice to a man)
tough joke

but actually I felt this inability
must be because I was so deeply wrong wrong

but back to Rick
the background blanketing of white noise mind
and over it, the song I sang:

"You don't want to do it? Fine.
You go ahead and do it.
You can't do it? Fine. You go ahead
and do it."

My gaze hovering just above his dick
the grey drywall behind, a half smile on my face
a Zen-like imperturbability
OMG LOL but straight up it was what I was going for
because what else to do

to cover the full-body cringe and cold sweat
the desire to run out of the room and beat my head
roll around on the floor, shaking my limbs
making sounds like, "Naahhhwaahhharghhaahhhhh!"

And failing that
I did all that but

in my head

and I didn't wonder what sort of effect
that could have on a person

"I love how you're so—"
Rick glanced at the ceiling, pausing, frowning
"how would you say it—

uninhibited."
His face melted into a lake of wonder
as he lingered over the breathy middle of that word

then sharp inhaled the butt end up
like a door, vacuum-closed shut (the sadness of that)

Ladybugs and Wishes

OK, so at a party with my housemate
I saw this girl, Cristina
in vintage minidress, white knee-high boots
and talking about how you worked the pole
twirling a fluoro feather boa
throwing her chestnut hair back
laugh rich like a river; later

I followed her to the bathroom line
gathered up the courage to tap her on the arm
said I'd heard her talking
and told her about the massage parlour. Well
her eye drills sharp
snap-dropped then froze as she
gutter-level shuddered

"God." She met my eyes like coming up for air.
"A rub and tug? At least *strip*. I mean get a *tan*."
She looked me up and down

"Then go strip somewhere. It's so much better.
Really. Those places are grope-a-thons."
Her sad urging eyes now
and one-side-of-her-face smile-contortion
the universal expression of pity, I thought

"Go to a *tanning salon*," she repeated
as though this was the solution to everything

and I nodded, as though yeah, I'll do that
because I didn't want to say
obviously there was no way I could strip
she was being funny, or mean
or who knew, suggesting it
the extra weight I was carrying for starters

and even if I was skinny
I mean when I *became* skinny
(the diet I was on that was gonna work
this time, remember)

all those eyes!
At the parlour I avoided doubles, even
and felt deficient because of that too

"Anyway it's only temporary," I said.
"After film school I'm out. I'm saving
for it now. It's in Vancouver."
I shrugged, like no big deal, but my grin
attacked my face and wouldn't leave
and I had the impression I was glowing

"Really?" she said.
"Well, you'll have to do something else there.
They don't have rub and tug
not like here. You'll end up straight-up hoeing."
"Of course they have it," I said.
"Who told you they did?"

God, what was her problem?
I was sure she was just raining on my parade
still, I'd ask Zu to be sure, she'd know

OK, so some weeks later, oh, joy
Cristina again, at another party
a pink bubble wand in her hand this time
an arc of pastel-ringed thought bubbles
I reached out to catch one
she asked what I was doing now, for cash

"The same," I said, but in a tone like
none of your nuisance business
and that's when the sad eyes came out again
then she gave some dude a lap dance
in the lounge room, in front of everyone

how I wished I was like her
wished I was her

The Deeper You Go, into the Ocean

But never mind, onto the next
sea vast with broom-like moustache
and voice like a speedboat
revving
telling me what I was going to do for him

seriously, I said,
we don't do that here; seriously he told me
the other girls were doing it
seriously, I said, no they weren't
but he said yes they were

"Shoulda picked one of them then," I said.
And not in my usual, soothing-chirpy tone
because he was wrenching at my boobs
like twisting stubborn jar tops
"Ow ow ow," I said, and seriously

where did they get these ideas?
"If you do that again I will leave."
The sentence popped out, Phoenix-
or Deja-style
I marvelled at it

and that's when he splutter-revved:
"Coming back with my boys
to kill you, whore!"

Well my stomach dropped
like in a bucket
plop

in my ears, running on pavement

in my hands, a towel
tying it around me with an attempted
casual-like smoothness
in case he was about to say he was joking

he didn't look like he was joking
but he must be, because seriously who

would react like that?
To not getting a blow job? By then
I'd been at the parlour almost ten months
and thought I'd seen everything

"You disrespect me!"
Like speedboat stuck in mud
the jammer and roar
and bulging eyes and neck
"You're a dead whore!"

The room dipped and buckled like a heat warp
my legs flooded, and still, what
was going on here
if this logically doesn't make sense
it can't be happening, right?
Yet I backed to the door

his face an ocean storm
my palm slipped off the doorknob
slick with oil
quick, use the towel
get it

his ragged shadow in the corner of my vision
sharking up off the table
I ducked out, raced down the hall
to the toilet

pressed against the door
my breath
in a trap
what a coward
and stupid
what if he has a gun, shoots through the door?
What if he shoots everyone?

Go out!
Go now

should have gone then
go
go now
why am I not

going
why am I not
getting to the phone
and calling the

police?
Why am I not
moving

muffled splutter-rev
and the higher pitches of girls
stomping then the jangle-jangle
of the front door opening
SLAM-CLATTER-CLATTER-jangle-jangle-
jangle-jangle ...
Hope

is a cold damp silence
waiting
breath
skating
over

a knock

"He's gone, come out."
Phoenix's voice

   then black leather and waist-length black hair
   an inch and an inch more
   a miracle, widening
   head tilted and wry smile
   like I was a floppy-eared puppy
   she had to clean up after.

"Maree, Maree. If he was going to kill anyone
would he tell us beforehand?
Would he *warn* us? Please."
She waved it away

   into the faux marble sink
   into the bucket with maelstrom
   of spray-bottle cleaning products
   into the hamper of thrown hotel white
   sheets and towels
   and washcloths

   the ones we held under hot water
   then took back to the room for them, after

   handkerchief-sized white rays
   with kite-like pectoral fins
   heavy with water
   and the spit-like parts of them
   they came here so violent to leave behind

Chariot

"Clients clients clients! And not enough girls!"

So they drove in and got me:
Zu and Tomasz and Deja
all the way from Bathurst and St Clair to Steeles
in a black SUV with tinted windows (a big deal!)
while talking about Andrea who'd lost her lease
or Erika who'd lost her mind
or Tanya who'd fallen asleep on a guy; "Zzzzzzz,"
Tomasz said, batting his palm against the wheel
head bouncing up and down in silent hysterics
"I mean, how do you *fall asleep?*"

"She do the body slide." Zu rolled her eyes
like that explained it
half turned around and held her painted finger up
then swiped it to the side
she knew we were doing them too, but OK

for girls like me and Deja, that is
not for everyone, and again I glowed
to be part of this in-group
and wondered why I was
then thought why not just be glad I was

while talking about who'd got stuck with a ticket
who'd gone to court, and who'd run out back
stilettos skating on ice, hid behind a dumpster
shaking like castanets (I imagined)
"Hey!" (Tomasz in a high-pitched voice):
"Did I get a ticket? No, bitches

I got pneumonia."
And laughter, because that did sound a bit like Tanya
and because it wasn't real pneumonia, Tomasz said.

"At least it wasn't an undercover," Deja said.
"Yeah," I said. "Real lucky."
As though none of these topics made my stomach
 drop, through the floor
pulped on the highway a few ks behind us already

"And that dope who always complains," Tomasz said,
"Donna didn't finish me, he tells me. I'm like, guy
what is *wrong* with you? I mean I talked to her
but. What does this joker want me to do about it?
I know he doesn't want me to do it for him."

Zu's crack-up like a cascade and windchimes
rolling down a staircase
and me giggling too, and feeling like wrapped up
and glad
they are on our side, I thought

also I was lifted out

of a cold windless day
and not knowing what to do with it
one of those days with a dead panic at the heart of it

or was the day not like that at all
pathetic fallacy
really pathetic! I thought, years later
before I'd forgiven myself

how I'd never learned how
to sit with an uncomfortable feeling
or feeling that was trying to tell me something
so

up up and away

in their chariot-narco truck, grasping the handle
foot on the step, memories of an above-ground pool
in a childhood backyard of fenced rage

the ladder resting against the curved blue wall
a deaf ear, as
"Stupid, good for nothing

the *Stupid Thing*," etc. etc.,
and on and on, telling me who I was
and who I would always be
"What you think doesn't matter
what you feel doesn't matter

you are a nobody."

I *know*.

When will it end when will it end when will
how to get out get out fly out
but there was no way out, then

but I would never be so trapped again, I told myself—

as onto Allen, onto Sheppard, floating high up
in their gas guzzler, environmental disaster
(as I didn't think of it then), feeling a part of
and a bit badass too
and when I told them I was leaving soon
for film school
Zu beamed

"Boyo, that's how you do it!"
She slapped her thigh. "I wish
you don't go. But I wish you do, too. Because *that's*
how you do it. That's why you do this
to get you where you need to go
then get out, that's it.
We've got plans too, Tomasz and me. Just a bit more
then we do real estate, all legit."

"Always a bit more," Tomasz said.
"But not always," Zu said. "Almost there.
This time we do it."

And she cast her hands out in front of her
flicking her red-tipped fingers out
like releasing fairy dust

gold scatter and star-filled in the dusk
the shimmering roofs of warehouses and strip malls
and tiny, mustard seeds of cars

II

II

Well I Got to Vancouver and All I Found Were Brothels

Yeah, so Cristina was right, and no
I hadn't asked Zu
or anyone else; figured
if I hoped hard enough it wouldn't be true? Well, turned out
unlike in Toronto, brothels were legal here
but massage parlours weren't (say what?)

and the only parlours I could find
were actually brothels. Big problem
I'd paid my tuition, but my whole plan to support myself:
parlours, and you know

I'd heard about those people who got their diplomas
while packing shelves, etc., every night
I didn't like to think about those people
what I knew: I wasn't smart like that
clearly I needed more time to study than they did
and my idea was to do well
so I could get a job after, and *start my career*

the phrase gave me goose bumps
like yes, then my life would start

but right now I needed money
to get me out of the hostel and into an apartment
already I'd been robbed from the first room I rented
by the man who rented it to me
which was why I was back at the hostel again
God oh God but no time to dwell on that
just no more share houses, I decided

no it wasn't possible for me do this brothel thing
this full service thing

but there must be a tip scale, right
like in the parlours?
Maybe I could do massages and hand jobs in a brothel
some of them might want that
especially if there weren't parlours here to go to for that
who knows
one way to find out

ii.

The manager now, but she'd been one of us, she said
and true, how she let her gaze play with your face like that
like she knew something you didn't
but she could tell you, maybe

she could draw it out …
And she gave us newbies advice, like:

"Don't mix the baby oil with the condoms
and don't let him get his dick in you too early
you won't last in this biz
watch out for the cokeheads and the assholes
they'll wear you out if you let them,"

and the place, which was named after a prominent figure
of classical antiquity
was much larger than Zu's place, and neat, and strict
the staircase outside was for smoking
high heels on metal, clanging like pots and pans
and visible from the street:
cocktail dresses and evening gowns at eleven a.m.,
no problem here, and yes
there was a tip scale:

hand job: $100
blow job: $200
full service: $300

in other words
I could just do the first one, right?
And maybe the second
not that I knew how to do that
although how difficult could it be
just gross, but less of a body invasion
I thought, than the third
and easier to make sure the condom was still on
safe sex, a principle that had sunk in
as a teenager when HIV entered public awareness
the Grim Reaper advertisement on TV

and on TV here: the nearby Vancouver Downtown Eastside
the HIV capital of North America, they said.

"Condoms for blow jobs too, and *always*," the manager said,
and phew! I thought. This made sense
when it came to blow jobs in general too
why would anyone do it without one, ever? But to the point:

at least now I knew most johns
(as some of the girls called them here
others called them clients, or jobs)—
would be happy to discover my amateur status so to speak
help a girl out with some advice. Double phew

so that was sorted, like a dusting of hands; done.
In contrast to Zu's smoky parlour
the air in here was fresh with a scent of mint
maybe I could quit smoking
and the music was low enough to read, good for studying
it was all going to work out! Ding-ding on the door
and for the line-up
we sat on a couch the size of small whale

took turns saying our names to the man who came in
legs to the side and together, never crossed
crossed looked "whorish" the manager said
with no indications of irony

fifteen (mostly White and Asian) girls
sitting cookie-cutter, smiling and making eyes
Stepford Wives eerie if you asked me
but no one did
and Monique told me only one Black girl allowed on shift
because White and Asian men were ninety percent of clients
and they picked White and Asian girls
ninety percent of the time, or so the argument went
"But how do they know that," Monique said.
"If there's only ever one of us here, to pick?"
And if you couldn't get shifts in-house
what was left was the street.

The first guy who picked me
wanted full service

I talked up my blow job, "The best you've ever had!"
LOL.
He walked straight over to another girl
and I went home with zero for my eight hours of sitting
so many girls on shift, and I was not one of the top girls.

"Don't worry hon," a girl in emerald told me.
"A lot of us don't like to do the lays.
But it's what most of them want, so."
And I watched, gaping (in my mind), at how she shrugged
sat down, pulled out her compact and dabbed her nose
applied more lipstick.
She had just done one.

My first was next shift
youngish, dark hair, not so tall. Hazy with blurred edges
tissue-rimmed with white

a man, a room, a wicker basket
with tall loopy handles (some Bible knitting companion
from the prairie?). Telling myself, "Relax, relax,"

self-talking myself, "Self, self,"
imagining open
front doors and entrances
drawbridges, sluice gates, truly, well
I guess it was a bit

funny?

?

Leaning back, back
into a place where I didn't have a body

(therefore nothing was happening to it)
I was just a mind
of pop songs or reciting things
the hook endlessly, playing

covering the puncture wounds in the silence deep as fangs

More than the Strangest Stranger to Me

       —But who was this 'I'? Was I
          Cartesian? (Did I think I could split 'em?)
          Hell yes

OK Miranda does have a body but she is not inside it
she is somewhere else

like in the umbrella holder
or neatly stacked shoe rack
by the front door
there is a spot
next to the melting mud slush or the hat that has

fallen; she is somewhere
there

Rent Day

And only one thing he'll pay for:

this man, balding, avuncular
the sort you could picture, aproned, barbecuing
while kids play in the pool, but it's me
whose blue

underwear around one ankle, like a soft cuff
and on the futon with smile like

my usual
what he can take it to mean: he's hot
the situation is hot, how could it be other
on the futon with smile like
looking forward to this; on the futon with

bile like, chartreuse and oxblood brown
wave breaks, the foaming
disintegration, throat-sharp and spilled-chemical
catastrophe

as he lowers his teeth

his front ones with the gap between
a sign of good fortune I'd been told
or maybe I read it somewhere
maybe in one of that brothel's
coffee table magazines; focusing on

details

that lead to thought flights; follow them; look
for more
where are they now

get out get out get out get out
OK then frantic pop songs pop songs
frantic

willing them to budge
the wall clock's frozen
face
when will it end when will it end when willlllll

please end please end please end
while I pretended to

enjoy it

sure it

wasn't convincing but no one

cares

(I pause on that fact now, like I didn't then)

how that's what
"I want you to enjoy it
OK," no question mark

means.

Propping myself up on one elbow
reaching for his dick
"Yeah, you want it," he says.
"Look how badly you want it,"

and, "Yes yes,"
of course I do
(get him off means get him out)
but his hands

pushing me back down
dragging it out
me laugh-pretending

"Yeah, yeah, you want me so bad."

Please end please end please end
I mean, "Mmm yes" and laugh-pretend

Red Velvet Suite

i.

Which is not to say it was all red velvet or that there was nearly
as much red, even, as I remember

not the classical antiquity place any more, this one a dive
my work visa had run out, and no
I had not factored that into my plans either
but no one had ever checked my ID at the parlour
also, I intended to call and renew my visa
that had to be possible; no way
I'd get into trouble over an itty-bitty

expired working visa, right? Hmm, OK
but in the meantime, you know
I wrote about the red velvet before, partially
in a short story, years later; well
I changed the city
changed it from brothel to escort, added
a cab ride, added two men, added roofies, you know

to make it *not my fault*

it was New Year's Eve, I kept that part
but did someone say that shift was "asking for crazies,"
then, or later? Was it the girl who told me she "worked on track"
and I thought what did that mean, maybe a drug reference?
But nodded and kept my mouth shut
so as not to look stupid, my MO
with time all new terms would become clear—so this girl

had long hair that was sometimes blonde, sometimes ginger
sometimes auburn, and she'd sit there hauling hair
between flattened palms slathered with straightening cream
tilting her head, a far-off gaze through the smoke haze

and over the top of the television, whatever
reality show or police procedural was spitting out of it
hair like an oil slick, but still she looked good, well
she was a pretty girl, with a round face and wide eyes
I wished I looked like her, I spent a lot of time

wishing such things, imagining
how I'd be loved if I looked like that
complete with glances and lines of dialogue and scenes
of adoration; that's

embarrassing isn't it, and a sorta big waste, then again
what else are you gonna do in one of these lounges
big laugh too (this girl had)
and if she didn't know what something meant she'd say so

often two guys would come in asking for her
sit in the lounge with us
leaning back, manspreading (as we didn't call it then)
one hand dangling in front of a dick, pointing at a dick
advertising a dick? Or a brittle

nonchalance; I never saw them take a session, hooker groupies
lookie-loos, dealers, or her pimps from the track?
Too young to be pimps I thought
but I knew nothing about pimps in the street sense. Her:

perched on the couch, tossing her head
talking and laughing about whatever like

people who can talk and laugh about whatever do
while the girl with the tortoiseshell mirror kept plucking
pluck pluck for hours (or so it seemed)
how you could see in here to do that, well
she did have striking brows
arches, vaults

and the third girl I remember
she'd arrive in cargo pants and shit-kicker boots
change into stilettos and a flouncy dress with frills and ruffles
she used to date a director who had some fresh fame at the time
I'd seen his last movie, an artsy parody; I was impressed
she told me about their life in New York
penthouse apartment and all the best restaurants
shopping sprees out of *Pretty Woman*. "For real," she said.
"Wish I'd kept some of that paper.
But that's the old story, right?" Well
usually three other girls on shift at that place
and these are three I can remember

but I don't know if that night it was these three.
My constant companion:
the plastic bottle with vodka and water
and powdered drink mix (diet)
but I wasn't at that time in the habit of getting wasted
while at the brothel I mean. Just that bit of alter
I needed. Shake it (my alter/altar)
watch the granules dust storm then

settle. Lift it to my mouth.
Feel the warm slow spreading like waves into sand
melt me into the foamy armchair, my bliss breath out

and that night we'd had champagne too because yippee
New Year's. 1999. That Prince song was everywhere.
I hadn't had a job yet when the man scattered in
like a cracked spigot. One of those young-old ones
with a face like a weatherboard house
skin stretched tight over cheekbones
tall, skinny, jittering
on something

but whatever. Sketchy as
but whatever. No it wasn't him but some other man, who
when I went out to greet

turned me around like a rotisserie
and I said, "All there?" Or:
"All in place?" But with a smile and a flirty laugh
as though I was chirpy-pleased, and he was hot. In any case
that guy didn't pick me. With the weatherboard man

I went into the room at the end of the hall.
My choice or his? (Sometimes they liked to pick that too.)
Maybe there were four rooms in this place, but I remember
only this room
with a futon that faced the window at the front; red (faux) velvet

curtains floor length. Outside the window was Hastings
I want to remember what it looked like from outside
there would have been a sign (red neon let's say)
and the front entrance that was on that street
a narrow flight of stairs like a bronchus

a sign then, a door, and a partial view
of a partial flight of stairs, I want to say
the door had a small square window at the top
and there might have been stair lights like ticker tape
missing a light every few, retroreflecting
up, up, let's say
a set of eyes could go
from a hypothetical car

window trailing caterpillar past in the night. Storefronts
boarded up. What
could have been seen from there was not
much, right
(velvet don't flutter)

maybe that's the point
from the front of the building these
were the things that didn't happen: the man wasn't

a tall hard shadow who shut the door behind him
and pushed me to the floor. And I didn't

feel the way I tumbled to be a soft cascade
(the hazy edges, and the white)

which is not how it must have been at all; it was also
a floor with carpet worn rock hard, like gum on pavement
and I didn't

laugh
because I always laughed, I wasn't acting, even at that point
as though this was funny and I was, as usual
delighted at whatever inane behaviour
wanting to move him to the futon
while keeping rapport, and I wasn't

pretending then, when that didn't work
(and pretending for whom?) that nothing was happening
that couldn't be sorted out
with more pretending
and not overreacting
but this man: like a swarm
of men. My throat burned exhaust and I knew

something was going wrong.

I said, "No,"
I said, "Please no." I said, "No no no."
I said, "At least not without a condom." What I didn't know

that a man could be a concrete block, a man could be an undertow
that I couldn't push him off, propel myself up
and what he kept

on going? Sorta disbelief, sorta struggle like inside
my skin like my skin
was a plastic bag to panic-wriggle out of, or a straitjacket; where

did my arms disappear to, then? Was he holding them down
maybe he wasn't, what was I doing with my (maybe)
free arms? It

took a long time, or
it was quick. He said some things or he said nothing
and made no sound, this
seems unlikely, where
were my ears? I was a smothering struggling in skin
what was happening, I mean what, actually
was this, was something I thought with an almost

intellectual curiosity (from way off up there, or over there, or
somewhere else); I mean, what, exactly
was happening here? I did not

yell. I did not scream

ii.

In which I went to a free clinic
in which I got tested. In which I said
I'd had 'unsafe sex'.
In which I filled out a form. In which
in response to the question:
"Have you ever been a sex worker?"
(Startled, and before I could think)
I answered: "Yes."
In which the man

pierce-glanced at me
then away (those eye drills again)
and I thought oh no, probably
you were supposed to lie about that

I never knew the correct things
to lie about, and I knew that I never knew
but knowing this didn't make me know.
Fear like an icy blanket, bucket stuffed
they'll call the cops!
It was legal here of course, but I wasn't

and in any case, there were harassments
or were these the easier worries to have
I don't know; worry like a

scurrying burrowing rat said keep
worrying yourself into the worry box
where worry thought worry was a way
to prevent that thing from happening
(let the gods know you were serious)
and see: all the tests came back negative
and no one came to arrest me. Crisis

averted, right? In which
I decided to leave the rest alone
like a gravestone I never visited
let the grasses and trees and
Spanish moss grow over
no, cover it with leaves
no, bulldoze it, no; in which

it returned to me (again again), as
images with no explanations
and because they wouldn't stop appearing
only thing to do was explain them
I mean try, I mean why
hadn't I fought back? I mean

more? What is a block what is an undertow
what was I doing with my, maybe
free arms? But then I'd start thinking
about things like the carpet

how thick it was near
those red velvet curtains
compared to the centre, crater
and how the dust and cobwebs
trailed from the curtain hem

a jungle world in miniature
with vines, creepers, lianas, epiphytes
I imagined myself, machete waving
aegis wielding
slashing my way through; this

seemed
funny?

And why I hadn't fought back
I mean more

I told none of the other girls
(I had a shower, went back
to the lounge, poured more champagne)

I told one man, months later
but said the guy was holding me down
then said he had a knife
shame upon shame

I was such a liar.

I thought:
if I tell it like I remember it
he won't think it was anything

and I wanted him to think
it was something

I wanted to tell someone
what I remembered
but when I tried what came out was

carpet
curtain
weatherboard
red velvet

and many years before I read
this is typical
of the way trauma can destroy narrative
the ability to tell one that is
in an A to B way, the fixation instead
on fragments, images
floating, cascading
trailing curtain dust

at the time
I put this down to my bad speaking skills
then proceeded to narrate
a version that fit better
with popular depictions
of what I called 'the r word'; this

made sense how? Years later too
I read that many of us come up with
a 'cover story'
meaning one we are able to tell
but back then, I couldn't understand
my lies, or those parts of the story
I could tell no one

and this too: that he left the money?
Wasn't even what they called
'theft of services'

iii.

"You can't rape a hooker,"

I heard that, years later
I mean I would have heard it at the time too
but I remember this one time I heard it
because I wrote it in my journal

it was on an episode of *Law and Order SVU*
it was not said by a sympathetic character
still, we know how lies can become truth
by being repeated
well I knew better but I also
didn't know better, you know, and

fight, flight—or freeze

it's a real thing, I know (now). Let's call that
a lightbulb that took approx. two decades
(to apply the idea to myself that is)
here's another:

wrenching at my boobs
like twisting stubborn jar tops
arm-eel flails and, "No no no,"
equals, "Blah blah blah,"
(aka a normal shift)
or silence deep as fangs
did I think, how
was this so different? Or

I could understand if it hadn't felt different
enough

to scream at least? Or there was some sort of
confusion as to whether it was different
that needed processing

in other words, time, which was not available
or, that in the moment, my learned default:
let it happen

let alone what
eye gouge, chokehold, knee to the groin
I'd never done anything like that; how
was I supposed to know how, right then?
And if I failed, would he hurt me worse
had that flown into my mind
I didn't know

I didn't remember feeling afraid
So I must not have been, right?
Wrong, but I didn't know that then

so back to it:
vines, creepers, lianas, machete
stumbling thought steps, red mud-stuck
shame-struck questions circling
really the same question
(again again), why

hadn't I fought back? I mean more

while the one I don't remember
ever thinking to ask: why did he do it

gaps in red
velvet curtains
peepholes of white
light

An Act of Glossing Over

or exonerating (not me, just my body)
or covering up (pop songs pop songs pop songs)
by means of a perfunctory
(hazy, so-called) *investigation*
(how it 'shouldn't matter'
according to me)

or thorough and biased
(didn't have to feel anything; why did I?
Other people would, so what did that make me
what I wanted to be, not human
like they thought too)

presentation of data (futon type
curtain colour, carpets)
an attempt to hide, or camouflage
(cocktail dresses, glitter, 'a job
like any other') *a liquid composition*
(the urge to run out of the room
hadn't left me; but reality:
you don't get paid if you do that)

a uniform glazed
appearance given (to put on my game face
I used to say, a session
being a session being a session

money in hand
and still in one piece?
OK then. Whatever happened in the room
it's all the same after, right) *to surfaces*

difficult to grasp (I made them that way too
because how to go on, otherwise)
that coats and smooths
(banter and laugh-pretend
women are for smiling

especially when suggested; reality:
you need to get paid) *bypass
discard overlook defer* (and avoid

wrath, male anger like a blood vessel
siren and hoof-beating stampede
stop it before it happens, you can't
but you try, but
sometimes you can, you even get good at it
you think, and you don't think

of re-enacting that trauma achieving that
mastery or exercising maladaptive defences)

over rough surfaces (what you think: pride
you found
your métier)

Circus Poem

—No, I was not an expert on myself

Black velvet with black and red lace, floor length
with thigh-high slit, discount-store special
vaguely goth funereal but for some reason, money
with faux diamond choker
silver glitter eyes and glitter brow—man
how I loved glitter, on anything

anyway, one night at the place on Hastings

one for Daisy, one for me
we all came out around the same time
talked and laughed about *COPS* episodes
in the lobby. After they left
me in the mirror:

lipstick smeared nose to chin; full clown mouth.

My hands clapped to my face and silent full-body
cry. Scrubbed it off like cleaning grout
then went to find Daisy: "Why didn't you tell me!"

"Don't worry," she said. "It wasn't that bad,"
without even asking what I was talking about
but it was really bad
I couldn't believe she hadn't said anything
often when I wore that dress I remembered

that part of the story

Head Shelves and Crawlspaces

The buzz on the door, the pop of vacuum
unsealing; hats, gloves, coats, peeling
the white water rushing
of steaming milk, the ruff-scruff on caramel
bristles of doormat, the background trip hop
with leaf-rustling rummage
static of newspapers
and fragments of what I called
'normal people conversation'; look

lookie-loo looking in windows you see the shiniest
of things, or looking at people as windows (open)
the flushed cheeks of the freshly arrived
the glance up and smile of the person opposite

a moment to imagine where they didn't
go at night, and what they hadn't
seen of men (I assumed; lookie-loo looking)
from a corner, with notebook open
pen running over pages and pages to say

what I'd seen, what I heard, what I thought
what he said, what I wished I'd said
and everything else I didn't even know

I wished I could talk to another person about.
Ink smudges on side of little finger and palm
periwinkle and Rorschachian, as I

into the spiral burning, pages
turning; how people went from one event to the next
with nothing in between?
If only I were so seamless, without this
necessity to record
'radioactive', I called my journals

later I bundled them in a plastic bag
sealed it with cummerbunds of masking tape
like a drug brick; stashed it

in case some random snooper
would be so interested! In discovering what
a terrible person I was? Not just what I did for cash
but what I had to tell myself, to crawl back into
a liveable headspace, crawlspace
scrawl place; pages

and pages of reassurance, from me to me
about 'how we' (me and I)
(sometimes I was on my side)
(a key weapon in any abusive relationship
is unpredictability) 'would work it out'

and how I wrote about 'fitting that into my head'
as though the latest happenings were creatures
with tentacles out for a strangling
spikes out for a stabbing

seven toed, dragon tongued, and slippery
as flippers, to grasp them
lift-shove them onto that head shelf
(the grappling, broomsticking skirmish
the helicoptering hand)

next to the other ones, slotted, catalogued
locked. Hands dusted, a clap to punctuate, and then

Gravel

Washington State near the BC border
squelching through puddles by the side of the road
down from the Denny's, I stuck out my thumb
and jogged over to a muddy sedan
a man in a mesh cap with a green fish on it
hair flurrying out the back like a hunk of tumbleweed

"What's wrong," he said, glancing at my face
so I sobbed out my story again, that is
the parts that covered my most immediate problem:

"Came on the bus to renew my work visa
they said come to the border and they'd fix it
but I got here and it wasn't true.
Refused entry back into Canada … my apartment
my money, my school … in Vancouver, what I need
to get back—"

The man pulled back onto the road
glanced at me again
but as though into the distance behind me as well.
"They lured you here, huh.
Told you to leave the country and come back in?
And you were dumb enough to do it?"

Fresh sobs bolted out. A guy at Denny's
had already offered this explanation
I couldn't believe this was widely known
"I didn't think immigration could, you know

lie to you like that."
The man thumped a closed fist on his thigh
and guffawed. "Cheaper for them! And less bother

yes sirree, than going up there and rooting you out
this way you do the job for them
now you're the US of A's problem. Yes sirree."

And he kept going on about it
like it was the funniest thing.
"Where are you headed?" I said,
hoping he wouldn't say all the way to Seattle
so I'd have an excuse to get out soon

Seattle—maybe I could start over there
did they have brothels, or maybe massage parlours?
I had enough money for a hostel for two nights
this plan was insane but what else to do
locked out of a country
locked out of a home
like losing your keys forever

"I'm not going far."
And he pulled into a parking lot outside a shop
an 'ICE CREAM!' sign draped in a US flag.
Stopped the car and turned to me.
His eyes were a pale iceberg blue
and I noticed again how his gaze took me in
but also seemed to diffuse around me

"It must be your dumb lucky day."
He told me he was headed back to Canada
he lived just over the border and did the trip often
a quiet crossing used by locals
no one asks for ID there, they wave you straight past
"But just in case, don't tell me your name.
We'll put your backpack in the trunk.
If they question me, you said you had papers
you're on your own," he stressed
"If they ask any questions."
I nodded, "Yes yes yes! Oh my God and thank you."

Was this even possible? "Thank you
thank you so much! I'd be so grateful."
He grunted. "You look like you've been crying a year.
In a gutter. Go wash your face at least."

The bathroom was one of those large square rooms
with a toilet and sink and dented hand dryer
smell of pee and sweat
and on the scuffed walls, Eliza + Mickey
and dick pics and boobs with smiley faces
I got out my plastic bottle
there'd been vodka in it when I'd left home
I'd had a good buzz on when all this started
maybe that hadn't been so smart either (ya think?)
although maybe it hadn't made any difference either
what I shouldn't have done in the first place
was get on that bus

I gripped the sink between guzzles of water
cupped more water in my palms
splashed it on my face, wondering how many others
had used this bathroom to gather up
some sort of temporary, workable self

as well as why drawing genitals
was so compelling to people

"That's better," he said, when I climbed back in.
"Not bad." His dispersed gaze dropped
radiated around my boobs this time. "Eat this."
He handed me a pink ice cream. "Strawberry. It's good.
I come here specially for it. The milk is different
this side of the border, did you know that?
Just sit there and eat it and try to look chilled out.
That's not how you look right now. Smile.
There you go. And don't speak
unless spoken to. I'll do the talking."

I nodded. I'd never been less interested in ice cream.
Still, I licked around the side of the cone
tilting my head, and held his gaze because

look, what I knew well by now
no man helped you for nothing

"Good, huh?" he said, smiling faintly
"You see what I mean, right? Creamier."
"Oh yeah."

I was imagining what they'd do to me
if they caught me trying to cross again
already I'd been promised a lifetime ban
on ever entering Canada if I showed my face
at that Peace Arch Border Crossing
one more time

and if they nabbed me at this outpost odds on
they'd toss me back there
and maybe with those same guys
the one with the red hair and nose like a crag
who nudged the other one in the ribs
pointed at his screen and whistled
spat out the name of that brothel on Hastings
how the hell
did they know about that?
Then I remembered the cop who came in once
and I was green enough to have my ID on me
and green-dumb enough to show it to him

but the manager said he hadn't run my details
sometimes cops came in because they were bored
or to gawk at hookers, they didn't actually run details
but I guess this one had

and these border guys
their hatred of everything they said I was
dripped from their faces
like saliva from the mouth of a rabid dog

then they put me in a holding cell
for what felt like forever
but was maybe a couple of hours
before handing me to the US cops, who arrested me
because they said I'd been in the US for a year
because I still had the green visa waiver slip
tucked in my passport, from when I'd visited Buffalo
I hadn't known I was supposed to hand it back
I didn't know how so many things could go wrong
and at once, and worse
the common theme: my stupid mistakes

well, after fingerprinting me and putting me in a cell
finally those US cops let me look in my backpack
for the bus ticket I kept telling them I had
it showed I'd just come from Vancouver.
"She's telling the truth!" One of them said,
  shaking his head in amazement.
"Hey bud, she's actually telling the truth."

So they put me in the squad car again
holding my head like a precious egg
then drove me to a section of highway
where they left me, at two a.m. or thereabouts
told me to make sure I left the US within three months.
I got my umbrella out of my backpack
thinking how absurd

the one thing I was prepared for was rain?
I walked towards the yellow and red sign
that blurred and hovered in the drizzling sky
it turned out to be an all-night Denny's
where I stayed crying until it was light

and now here I was, with this man
who said his name was Bob; oh God
I didn't want to see those Peace Arch guys again
if they sent me back there

please God please God, I whispered in my head
as we slowed and pulled up to a small box
like a tollbooth. "Hey," I croaked
and waved at the guard, then gah
I wasn't supposed to say anything
the second any word with an 'r' in it escaped my lips
I could no longer pass for North American.

I licked the ice cream
then quickly returned my hand to my lap
I was shaking too much.
The guard lifted himself off his seat
peered into the car. I glanced at my chest
which was thumping and trembling
like rocks hurled from inside my ribcage
any moment he'd notice
and holding my breath made it worse

please God please God
and I wasn't sure who this God was
but my praying was louder than what Bob
and this border guy were saying

please God please God
heart beating in my ears
sweat piped from my underarms
the ice cream cone slippery in my fingers

then under me
movement

the box with the guard sliding out
of the side of my vision
in its place, trees
sliding like still holding your breath

glimpsing the possibility
of freedom
but not yet
because maybe just into that bay

for further questioning? Please pass that bay please
pass that bay please God who I didn't know who
or what this God was
almost past
like one monkey
two monkey

God and monkeys
please make it so, and now

we were past that bay
now we were back on the highway.

I turned around
gulping in breaths
every metre, a metre further
into Canada, bit more
bit more

how much more before I could believe it was true
that no one would call us back
God and melted sticky pink talcum powder ice cream

"We made it," I gasped. "We made it!"

"Told you. No problems. Although I thought
you were fixing to blow it. What were you doing
speaking? All you had to do was sit there.
That's why I bought you the *ice cream*."
Bob scowled at the mess in my fingers.

"Sorry, it's ugh." I opened the window and tossed it.
"That's grand now," Bob tsked.
"Get us pulled over now, for littering."
"Sorry. I did look around first. It's clean waste anyway."
"Clean waste?"
"Animals will eat it." I wiped my hands on my jeans
in case asking for tissues might be another misstep.
"What animals?"
"We made it!" I said
and I could have said it a hundred times

because we made it we made it we made it
but of course, it was me who'd made it
the miracle was mine, not his
maybe he felt left out. "Thanks to you!" I added
and "Thank you thank you."
"Yeah." He grunted again, and I took him in
more thoroughly now, as a person
not just a means

of getting back over the border (maybe).
A raised mole the size of a dime
dangled from the side of his neck
like a small brown ear
ringed with red
should he get this checked out? Should I
suggest this?

"You realise no one knows you're in the country?"
He scratched the mole with a dirty fingernail
as though he knew I'd been thinking about it.
"I mean records will show you tried to get back in
but couldn't."

I nodded. I'd have to deal with my school to start with
or would I? Would they find out?
Yes, as it happened

(they found out about the immigration violation
I was never sure about the rest)
in any case, I wouldn't graduate

too scared to come in for the last two weeks of classes
in case they were obligated to turn me in
so I failed my attendance requirement

too ashamed to come in, also
in case they knew about the rest
and even though one school employee
was a buyer at the brothel
he'd picked me, a couple of times
and male classmates boasted
about getting escorts on the regular
but I was too ashamed

if I'd known that then
that everything that had happened in Vancouver
turned out to be *for nothing*
as I saw it
but I didn't know any of that then; what I knew:

first thing I needed to get home, sleep, recover
home, home!
Whereas before it hadn't seemed like much of one
now it was the best, and all I wanted

I fell into imagining what I'd do first
shower right; no, coffee then shower; no vodka then
coffee then kiss that peeling kitchen parquet
lie on my back
make like a snow angel
thank my stars
vow from now on I'd be grateful for everything
I saw myself there right now

soaping off the filth of this whole ordeal
breathing in steam, breathing in safe
the apartment door locked
security chain in the slot
safe, safe

and so it dawned on me, slow, slow
that the car had slowed
that Bob was turning off the highway
bringing me back: the lurch

and gravel crunch-punch.
"Er. Er—where are we going?"

"I want to show you something," he said,
too crisply, as though he'd rehearsed that line?
"Oh, that's OK," I said. "I don't need to see anything,"
as though he were asking for my input or opinion.
But of course, he wanted me to make good
on what I had not forgotten I'd half promised
although I'd hoped now that I was across, he'd forget
or I'd skip out of the car at a traffic light or a stop sign

thank you and see you later!
Except my backpack was in the trunk.
I wanted to keep my keys and ID
and now we were off the highway
and heading further off

"Look," I said. "I appreciate you taking me over.
I'm so appreciative. If you want we can sit
and you know, talk. OK?"
I risked touching his grotty plaid sleeve.
I hoped he'd be happy with a hand job only.
Just like in the brothel or the parlour, right?
Only here my payment was not money
but safe passage

but find a reason to get my backpack first
have it next to me
so I could leave straight after
or make a dash for it if he went for more
or just sprint as soon as I got my backpack?

"This is too far off the main road," I said.
But if you'll go back. OK?"

I kept leaning forward and looking at his eyes
trying to get him to look back at me
but he didn't, and he kept on driving

now what? What could possibly be happening
now? And I stayed stuck on that
how after all that had already happened
something new and bad could not be happening
but really, I had the feeling
something was going
wrong

but OK, I self-talked myself, "Self, self,"
dude is a bit weird
is all. You're back in Canada at least
he'll show you some duckpond or whatever
he'll turn around in a minute, and as though
it was not really happening

until
and
unless

I admitted it to myself in words.
He slowed and turned off again
onto a road that ended in a small gravel bladder
surrounded with trees. Cut the engine, the keys
clinked like champagne toasts then clackety-tack

of the door opening
soft padding footsteps
the crack of the trunk

why was I still sitting here? Go!
Opened the door and scrambled out
but he was already there.
Holding my backpack in front of him
like a boxed gift I was not meant to take

and he stood there like that
his gaze taking me in, and whatever was behind me
the driver's seat, the woods

too far from help now, I knew
say something say anything
so I opened my mouth and blabbed
about the wife and the kids
repeating the stuff he'd said that I didn't know
I'd paid attention to, pretending to listen
I thought, so he'd like me, so he'd take me over

but turns out there was a model car and a garage
that needed sorting and a son
who was taking off training wheels
and they're going to do that today
when he comes back with the ice cream
and how much they like this ice cream too
all packed up in the cooler for them
little Scotty you know, waiting for his ice cream
and bike-riding lessons, from his great dad …

He sat my backpack on the ground
half straightened up, reached for it again
then changed his mind again

my legs sparked
my legs were rivers
my legs were gone
but ready to go

but where; could I outrun him?
His hands were empty by his sides
but did he have a weapon somewhere?
In his jacket pocket or where? What did he want?
What was he going to do?
What was I going to do? I

kept saying their names

the two kids, Scotty and Annie, and how great
to have a family, I'd do anything to have one
it was all I wanted in the world, and he had that

say things and keep saying them

his iceberg eyes
the gravel bladder, the luminescent glow, pure
adrenaline injected the trees with
greener than green dye
the sky with bluer than blue. He dropped

his gaze. Kicked the dirt. Cleared his throat
like sludging his voice up from a depth

"Gutter trash," he said. "Not even worth it."
Then he strode back to the driver's side
I grabbed my backpack, jolty-legged stepping, back
the spark of the engine
the sedan floated like brown flames
at the top periphery of my vision
as I kept my eyes trained on the ground
as though if I looked at him or his car directly
whatever spell had been cast to end this would burst

if the spell were like a bubble, which it might be
as puncture-fragile as that, and afterwards
there would be no way to say it had ever been here

don't look up don't look up

tyres popping over gravel and engine fading
like gurgling rain
I waited until all I could hear was my breathing
through rubber lips, mouth
stuck to my swallow

hugging close to the trees
I waded through the long grass
bolts in my chest at the twigs
that cracked under my sneakers

stone still to listen
then starting out again

back at the highway I stuck out a shaking thumb
self-talking myself, "Calm down
calm down, self, self,"
get a ride first, you can't hang around here
what if he changes his mind, comes back
calm down, calm down, self, self

it's all OK, or it will be
but it could have happened again, or worse
but it didn't, but it could have
but it didn't, but I couldn't stop hearing that
how it could have it could have it could have

III

III

Home Sweet

i.

So I went back to Toronto, and you know
I could have gone back to Zu's place
I saw it advertised, same number
in the crammed (what people called) 'adult'
section, back pages of *Eye Weekly* this time

but I couldn't pick up the phone
couldn't tell her where I'd been
and why I didn't graduate
and I didn't know how to lie about it either
I wondered what had happened
to her plans to leave
then decided I didn't want to know

and you know, I could have
gone to some other parlour
but I didn't care what I did any more
(a session being a session being a session)

and so I put a neat red circle
around an ad for an escort agency
picked up the phone and dialled

thinking how absurd I was doing this now
should have done it in Vancouver already
the cops rarely bothered escorts
since sex was already included in the price
no extras to negotiate for
(at least not for me; vanilla me)
meant no discussion of services for prices
meant nothing to bust anyone for

and straight from my apartment to the driver
to the john, meant you weren't sitting in a room
with a bunch of other girls
for easy immigration checks
probably I'd never have been found in escort

but back then I'd been afraid
to go into men's homes
who knew what was waiting for you there
but turns out you show up once
and it's easy after that (the showing up

at least, is easy). Drink from your vodka
in the car, then faux strut in your boots
the night will shelter you

and the hotels were even easier
neutral territory, and cleaner
and sometimes real nice hotels

real nice hotels were my favourite places
felt like you could pretend you were someone
going somewhere in life
even just walking through them

and you could pretend so well
felt like it was true; well at first

I was staying at Sylvia's
while I saved money and found an apartment
one that would take me
since I had no job I could put on an application
and no income I could prove
I envied Sylvia with her admin. assistant job
and funky loft on King West
with what they called rads
I loved how they belched heat

the roasting windowsill
and snow that collected on the other side
like white whales breaching

Sylvia knew what I did to get money
and usually didn't mention it
until one night she was tipsy.
"Don't you go to restaurants?" she said.
"Maybe I could do it too, like on weekends.
It might be hot." And so I had to explain

in terms of the agency I was at, anyway
(and even in the nicest of the real nice hotels)
let's say ninety-five per cent of the time
not escorting anyone anywhere
and my answer: "I *guess* you could say no

but it would be weird. You won't get paid
and you'd have to explain why
and it'd want to be plausible,"—well

stunned stonkered eye drills
with overlay of bitten on hairball
frozen jawed waiting to spit it out

I was out every night after that
got that apartment quick

ii.

Once I got a job as an office assistant
at a corporate video company
a big deal! Not exactly 'in film'
but in the neighbourhood, and interesting
compared to the waitressing and retail work
I was occasionally able to lie my way into
with invented CV experience

mostly I did this after a bad john
at which time I'd swear off escort
and this whole stinking industry, forever

only to get fired from the job for no-shows
the alcohol benders that were mostly
replacing the food binges
although sometimes it was both
the alcohol first, then the food
to tamp down my hangover, and mortification
or grief, over what I'd done drunk

like losing an envelope with a week's earnings
set aside to pay bills; carrying it around
rather than leaving it in my apartment
with its dinged-up door
and half-falling-off lock, and the man
who had an apartment down the hall
pounding on that door and screaming
that I was a house thief.
"He used to think my apartment was his,"
a neighbour told me.
"I guess now he's moved on to yours."
One day the psych. ward came and got him

to torture myself further, maybe
I remembered each john from that week

for zero dollars in my hand
and zero bills paid, and I could never believe

I'd done it again
(the drink or the food)
and I was never, ever, doing it again
until I did it again
often that same day

and even when I did show up
at those waitressing and retail jobs
seriously almost in tears of boredom

like I didn't know who I was without
a level of danger and crisis
the silence howled
an itching panic, and a mourning
and this thought:

two or three eight-hour days
in the tears-of-boredom jobs
or one hour (or less) with a john?

For shame! I knew I was not a good person
but this video job, OK! I wanted this job
I thought. My lack of graduating aside
I was beginning to suspect I was not cut out
for a career in film production anyway
what I'd liked best about film school
was sitting in a room alone
writing the short screenplays
but this job

it would be something film related at least
and I got the impression, clear tasks
and if you'd done everything required
I was sure they'd allow you to read
(no staring into space necessary); OK

my first day of work
I got on the bus
in a navy-blue suit, bought for the occasion
not suede, but a suit I could imagine
Lisa wearing, and sure, I thought
I could pretend this was back then too

that none of the events of the last year and a half
had happened
I was starting from now

why not? To merely live in this world
was to buy into far more outrageous fictions.
I'd just have to learn that computer program
I couldn't even remember the name of now
but I told them I knew it
like Sylvia said: "You say you can do it
then you pick it up, on the job,"

because you are such a bright shiny person
like she is, right, who picks things up
but I knew I was not, but I'd try to be this time
but what if I couldn't?
I still didn't own a computer
and only barely knew how to use one
let alone this program
but maybe they'd have a manual
maybe I could work it out; OK

OK, but what about my CV
with the film school graduation
what if they checked, oh God

what if they rang the school?
And the school told them about the brothel?

I leaned forward and yanked at my coat
fumbling my arms out of the sleeves
(pressed in against the window seat)
ripped off my hat, my scarf
sweat prickling my arms, my back
oh God oh God

probably they knew everything already
they were just waiting for me to get there
so they could tell me what a terrible person I was

and even if they didn't know yet
they'd find out eventually
and then: the sniggers and stares
and the fact that I hadn't thought of

any of this, until now
was unbelievable
but also typical, wasn't it
I never thought of things when I should
I was so stupid

stupid, which was what they were
waiting there to tell me, stupid and a liar
and a whore
a disgusting human

I sprang to my feet
stumbled past the woman next to me
as she hurried her legs into the aisle
then flailed through
the blotchy shapes shimmering

got off the bus
went home. Later
I told a couple of my bar friends about it
sort of:
"See I got a whiff of the commute already
decided it wasn't for me." It got lots of
drunk laughs

and so I went back
to that place where I knew what to do
and how to do it
it was always there to catch me
and wasn't that what a friend was
what a home was?

On Jarvis

And the girl who kept on, whisper-shouting
"You can't pick up a girl here!" And the driver
who kept on saying, "Why not?" And the girl
who kept on not saying
because it's right on the stroll, you moron!
Kept saying: "You can't pick up a girl here
you can't pick up a girl here
you can't

does he know any of our real names?
I am on parole." And the driver's strangled
"Why not, why not?" And the cop at the window
tapping; I was in the back seat

with the one on parole
stuffing condoms and baggies into the seat pocket
trembling under her jacket with studs and spikes
and the other girl in an evening gown
sequins and low-cut
coat falling away from one shoulder
one of those blasé-about-anything types
or high, not sure, making eyes at the cop

before his flashlight made her turn her head
and scrunch up her face
then I did the same
the black lightened and flickered black again
like a lighthouse searchlight

"Licence and registration please," the cop said,
and the driver opened the glovebox
his twitchy hand rifled through

emerged with a dog-eared piece of paper
and his licence from his wallet
a pause

then the cop peered in at the back seat again
running his eyes over the three of us
while he chewed his lip

crackle-bark of muffled voices
like a channel scramble with beatboxing pouring
into the silence of the black velvet night.
He straightened up.
"Got it," he said
into the walkie-talkie at his collarbone.
He held out the licence and the dog-eared paper.

"Don't make any more pick-ups along here, OK."
Then brisk footsteps, away

I turned my head to look out the back window
the blue and red pulsing
sharked out and melded
with the lights and the cars on the street
in front of us now
silence

until the burst:
"Phewwww!"
Then laughing, sighing
and the one on parole, "Goddamn
something better than us must have come along
and *right* then. We were screwed

goddamn." And the blasé girl snorting
"Nothing for them to charge us with!"
And the one on parole, "They don't need
anything, they can make it up,"

and the one in the front (the pick-up)
I can't remember, and the driver
didn't say anything, but I felt his dank panic
the type of panic that doesn't go away
when its trigger fades from view
when everything is *all right* so to speak
because it was my own

Why We Are Girls

>—(Or ladies, sometimes, but everyone
> knows that's a bit funny)

A girl is a wisp, a potato chip
barely there, a girl drifts
by the side of the road until you show up
then she's happy to do whatever you want
more than that: she's waiting
for the opportunity, any time, any place
she's a good-time girl

(your good time that means)
and when with you, the others don't exist.
You don't have to love a girl although
you can pretend to if it gets you off
since that's the most important thing, always
and you can pretend so well
you believe it; you can

do whatever with whoever but the girl
only does it with you, this is true
even when it's obviously not true
see above re pretending; you

don't need to sell this fantasy to a girl
she's already been sold it
and is ready to reflect it back to you
(which doesn't mean she's bought it
or it could mean she has, too). Cash
or cash equivalents are involved
but you can pretend she'd do it for free

if she could (you even say that
and she smiles and laughs
so you know it's true)

"You like that don't you," you
do not need to put a question mark
on that. A girl always says yes
or smiles and laughs, which is the same
as a yes, or squirms and looks like she
doesn't want to be there; that
just means she's *shy* (bonus for
you!) and is a yes too. A girl is

younger than you no matter what age she is
although obviously it's better
if she's actually younger. You
are the boss even as you like to
tell her she is (many of you
preferred it that way); tell her about how

empowering all this is for her
she loves it. A girl has no vital
functions you need to know about.
She's a roadside attraction with heart-shaped
shades that reflect your image
sucking on a red lollypop or awkward
urchin type with acne and hand-me-downs
plain, tattered, or refreshingly
unadorned, yeah. A girl

naturally just is whatever you want
her to be; amazing, right? Even when
she's not, for those who like
a bit of a challenge, or the troubled
ones, the ones who need
rescuing (to all the Captain Save-a-Hoes)
or the ones who won't be rescued
the hopeless cases

they're so romantic, dead
by the side of the road
you can faux mourn them.

Mr Donut

A brothel run out of an apartment
a high-rise near a major subway station; places like that
were just asking to be busted
(the neighbours don't like it)
later I saw it on the news, but for a drug ring

what I remember: a circular driveway and dried-up fountain
with verdigris bowl and cracked Grecian sculpture
grasses and vines grown over
boxed intercom white noise and slam of the steel door
then up a brown corridor, into a room that floats

in front of a balcony
hexagonal wire and a cloud of fur?
A blown-out photograph whisked in front of my face
and again
but never long enough
to say for sure

rabbits? And an idea that there was a baby too
(a human one), but was that
this apartment, or some other? Trying to dig to the truth
of memories like this, it doesn't get me anywhere

but the itch, once scratched
hard to leave alone, and I think
(little addict me)
this time, maybe, I'll get through, but not this one
not this baby, but an apartment hallway

does arrive, with amber parquet and rectangles like fingers
stacked in squares (was that this
hallway?). Here's what I think I can pin down:

the room on the right, the futon
the man in the checked jacket, orange and brown
a gold necklace snaking through chest chair
acne scars on his cheeks like raindrops in puddles
I must have given him my number

because after I'd quit that brothel
we'd meet at his donut shop
and he'd drive us to his house in Etobicoke
his wife visited her mother on weekends, he said.
Pictures of the wife, long hair framing her heart-shaped face
and wide warm smile; why
would he cheat on her with me? I thought
and felt embarrassed about
that aspect? Yeah, I *know*
but I didn't then, not quite; well this man

one of those who liked to pull out hunks of silver and gold
shove watches under my nose
gesture at dining room candelabras; affix dollar amounts.
His low-roofed house, cluttered as a tchotchke emporium
plus he never tipped me
and often counted out the last ten in loonies and toonies.
"You are the best,"

he'd tell me, "For sex …"
And with that pause, after
every time
maybe meant to be half of what he wanted to communicate
like, You are the best, for sex … *but:*

no good for whatever else? But he never added anything
so maybe just mantra-reassurance
that I was money well allocated

the best product at the best price. I smiled and laughed
(of course). This may have been the extent of our
conversation. He liked to sit with me in the donut shop

before we went to his house
he wanted his employees to see me
he said, for them to know he had a *mistress*

(if they thought he was paying me that was good too
or better, not sure); too bad
this bunch of nonplussed artsy types
didn't appear interested in anything their boss was doing
whenever I went there I wanted to talk to them
but I didn't know how.
One time I showed up in a brown leather coat
I'd bought at Kensington Market
worn soft, with scuffs like floating continents
whole other worlds; well

Mr Donut (as I called him, to myself)
went straight to his car, an SUV
beige, with dark brown coffee cup holders
(is that a real memory? Was that this SUV?)
and waved his hand in short quick stabs
for me to get in. "No *mistress* of mine,"

he said, "Should wear *rags* like that."
"It's vintage," I said, but then felt red and hot
arrows and pinned to the seat, mumbling apologies
into my lap. How I hated to displease anyone
and hated myself even more, for hating this

next time, I thought
I'd tell him where he could stick his opinion about my coat
but instead I just wore the white coat

I Am

I am the opposite of his wife, I am like some old girlfriend
he could have married, I am like an affair he just had
I am not at all like the last girl who showed up; I am
exactly like her. I am the first tall girl he's had
I am the first girl with long legs, I am the only girl
with real boobs, even if they're too small/he prefers asses
why don't I get some work done, it's great
I haven't had any work done
it makes me different. I am the only Australian he knows
he knows many Australians but none of them look like me
where else is my family from, ah, Germany
that explains it, I look German to him
I should say I'm German, it's more accurate, besides which
Germans are tall. I am really not that tall. Pale though
I am the palest girl he's seen, I should get a tan
I should stay exactly as is, he loves pale skin. Am I sure
I'm not Irish? I am a bit like an Irish girl he used to know.
I am a nice girl, he can tell, from a good family; what
am I doing here? Wait, don't tell him.
It's none of his business. Probably I have children.
And a pimp? Wait, don't tell him. Probably
I've been raped. Wait, don't tell him. Obviously
I was molested as a child; will I give him a
girlfriend experience? What's wrong with me?
What difference could it make to me?
He's a clean guy. He can tell I want him, all women do
look at him. Countless hours in the gym right there.
I am a whore, I am a nympho who loves everything he does
don't I always say so? Especially when prompted
but that's because I'm shy. A shy whore nympho
I can't get enough, being paid for what I'd be doing anyway
I'm a fucking genius! I should be paying *him*! (Hahahaha

he knows I've never heard that one before.) But why
won't I fuck without a rubber? Clearly
I'm not too bright and don't have an education.
That was a half-assed fake if he ever saw one. I am a liar
pure and simple, a dishonest person, isn't that why
I call him a trick? There's extra in it for me if I'll
"lose control, go completely *crazy*,"
it will prove to him I am the whore he says I am.
I am pure fun, I am a bit too serious, I am complex
I can be read like a book
I am a free spirit, with the world on my shoulders
stereotypically tragic, I could be rescued, I am too far gone
I am not noteworthy at all; who would bother?
I am a topic for discussion and analysis. I am paid
like various famous people have said, for leaving after.
Promptly, if I don't mind. Various famous people are morons
what he likes to do is cuddle, please stay. I am a handful
he is sure. Street-smart and ruthless, I am sweet kind sugar
awkward and klutzy, I am smooth as glass.
Naive and gullible, I am a smart businesswoman
with "all the power," I am a hellion
with flashes of the devil if he believed in Him:
I am a picture of what he wanted
I am not what he was looking for at all

He Is

He is an out-of-town businessman, he is a downtown
businessman, he is on his lunch break/dinner break/holiday/
after hours, he is a hedge fund manager, graphic designer
non-profit; he is out there in winter on power lines
he can show me the frostbite scars. Mumbling and blushing
he reaches out, twig-like and afraid
frenzy-pouncing, he shoves my head onto his dick
grabs me by the hair, by the neck. Poking me
like the buttons of an unfamiliar or dangerous
or fascinating or boring machine
he describes the type of girl he likes, who is nothing like me
he says I am wonderful, he says I am just his type
he says he is filled with shame. Straight up, he says
he is on coke, I could be here a while.
Luckily an hour is an hour is an hour
but this hour will not be thirty-five minutes. Nope
he's done in fifteen, I can go. He is a clock-watcher
who spends most of the time arguing about the time
and does not appreciate any irony being pointed out
with respect to this, and howls like a toddler
when I say I'm leaving unless he ponies up for more.
Other girls ask him if he works for free in his job
but I don't, I know this is not actually a job like his
but more importantly I prefer not to cause offence
or risk retribution, and politely decline a personal cheque.
He has two kids asleep in the hotel room, "Shh!"
Can I piss on him in the bathroom?
His family is long gone, he's an addict spending it all
on massage girls and hookers and booze and blow.
He's received a diagnosis, so why not. His wife left him
this is her money he's spending, so why not.
Nothing special has happened to him lately

so why not. He is anti-drug, he is a teetotaller, he is in AA
he is not in AA, but should be
(I can call it when it comes to others)
he is anti-feminist, he is the biggest feminist I'll ever meet
"Let me tell you," (all about how)
"women should use their bodies as they please
now where is that girlfriend experience?" You know
the one who does everything he wants
whatever it is, always, and loves it; that kind of girlfriend.
He is a man who rates races
based on the physical attractiveness of the women
according to him; it's something he spends a lot of time
thinking [sic] about, and discussing with other men
in internet forums, increasingly
a horrific development (the internet forums, that is
the racism is business as usual). He is a man
who makes offensive comments about every
marginalised group you can think of
because who am I going to tell
or maybe it's just his normal conversation. He is a man
who makes sick comments about children. Usually
I switch (all these) subjects. But sometimes
I let him rattle on; tune out
because whatever gets him off quicker so I can leave
is what I'll do; I get a sick feeling in my mouth
when I do this, which I 'solve'
with more vodka; he is a man who hounds me
to "*make sure* I enjoy it,"
he will not stop ranting on about it
and my best fake will not satisfy him, although admittedly
I think my best fake is not very good
I feel embarrassed about this? Not sure if for me or him
or both, but see above re vodka; he is married
with a boring life, he is married with a full life
he is married with a wife busy with children
a wife who stopped wanting sex

a wife who is having an affair, and has given her blessing
for him to do the same, and a wife
who has no idea (mostly), but who, if she knew
would regard a hoe as less hurtful than an affair
because of the absence of emotional involvement, he says
"Now can we fuck without a rubber?"
He is a doting overworked man with a sick wife.
He wants me to know he "never does this,"
and he really has never done this (before me; occasionally
this is true). He is a bright shiny man
heading a clean water project, criminal justice reform
and counselling at-risk youth; I wish I had his life
or could be his friend, for real. He is a scholar, he is a judge
who has "given it to whores" in thirty states
and I can't remember how many Canadian provinces
but he was getting to all of them
"Some of us," he says. "Have to have goals."

Aquarium

White lines like white gills on black sea
of Ramada, information binder
next to the fist-crumpled cans of Molson
rumpled maple leaves
and punched flat du Maurier packs
their blackened lungs and old corn teeth
and Stan:

forehead glistening like bubble wrap
as he tapped the rolled-up bill
rat-a-tat-tat, then flipped it between two fingers
held it out to me. "In a few hours,"

he said, "it will be the worst day of my life.
And not just the worst day, the worst day *again*
you know what I mean."

Well I nodded, but thought
why should I know what he means?
Sure, first thing I'd tottered into the bathroom
chugged from the vodka in my purse
and flushed the toilet to pretend I'd used it
like he was paying attention or cared
and that's when I spied the trash

a graveyard of bent and twisted
eggnog and beige body bags
in between tissues like scrunched sheets

"After this I'll be back at the ATM,"
he said. "Take out the rest of my overdraft
then across the park, find my dealer
then ring another agency, you know
my *other* dealer

you're great but no offence
you could be the best in the world,"

he paused and stared at the thick beige curtain
imagining, maybe
what the best whore in the world would be?
I mean what would that
entail

or was he just zoning out

"The point is not the best."
His gaze snapped back to me.
"The point is another."
"I get it," I said.

"I know you do. And I'd be embarrassed
to call you back, see I'm embarrassed
but not too embarrassed to tell you I'm
embarrassed, what kind of
embarrassed is that
but we're used to it aren't we, addicts
the worst day of my life! In a few hours

all my money will be gone, I mean all
and nothing I can do to stop it
I used to try, you know, white-knuckle it
anything I could do not to give in."
He touched his clenched fists to his forehead
knuckles facing me
shook his head. When he pulled his fists away

a clump of hair stood to attention
like a honey-hued fin

his eyes, lit like torches
and dead like the night
the one we can't see beyond those curtains

"You know they say wait, and the urge
will leave? Well, it never did
it kept at me and at me
until I said you win. You win every time
so I thought why not cut that middle part out
the trying not to, that extra suffering
that doesn't make any difference
now when it comes on I just
go

since it's what will happen anyway
I used to work on Bay Street
on a Y2K project you know
80K a year!
Can you believe it? Fancy-assed condo
rare fish in the lobby.
Like hundred-dollar fish or some shit.
Watching them go round and round. Round
and round. What a life. If I stopped now
I'd have a roof tonight, but I won't stop now

you know how it is
I'm only telling you because you know
there's no point telling anyone who doesn't.
They don't get it; may as well talk some
whole other language."
Well, at this point I was like, Stan

I'm not the one who's gonna be homeless
in a few hours, so ask yourself
(I wanted to ask him), what
is it you think I know?
I hadn't binge eaten for months
so far as I was concerned, zero *harmful*
addictions going on in my world

but his gabbing aside, he was an easy call
how he stroked my hair
the familiar and reassuring taste of latex
like rubber tree and pool toys
filling my mouth.
He said, "Ahhh …"
He said, "Thank you."
Then pulled away, enough
he was exhausted

it was all he'd been doing for three days straight
coke and hookers
the guy was done in

the guy needed sleep, the guy needed a mother
the guy needed a couple of twelve-step programs
is that what he thought I knew? Others like him

and true: in this situation I was
one half of his addiction
supplier, pusher, even

as well as moderate, OK, but still
co-consumer of the other half
even if it was just to be social
not to wreck my booze and Valium buzz
when I got home
the Valium that was only at home
and only at the end of the night
that buzz that was really an off switch
but fully under control

I set the rolled-up bill back on the info binder
watched how it jolty swelled
then slowly, unravelled

bit more, until it came to a pause
a green paper finger, and I felt the weight
of (all) that sinking
in

but buck up, what
was it I wanted me to do here? To leave
before I collected all the cash this Stan was most
willing to give me, went against everything
I'd learned over what was still such a tender
amount of time, to feel like a lifetime

plus, look what those others had done to me
in parlours, in brothels, in high- or low-end hotels
on a bus, at a landlord's house
in a doctor's office, etc.—

and then there was the red velvet.
Getting mine, wasn't I
for all that
which was not Stan's personal fault
and probably he never did any of those things
but too bad, so OK
we'll try a different tack; what

could I do? That paper was sinking all the way
to the bottom of the tank. Someone
was gonna be there to scoop it up; why not me?

Money: Some (More) Points

i.

Once I put a stack of bills on the bed
smeared them around
rolled in them. Then I gathered them back up
recounted them.
I didn't bother doing it naked. I was alone, anyway

ii.

The smell, like refrigerators after rain
a soft fork to the ribs, or inflatable eyes, breathing
a graspable weight, like curtains or toast
to cradle in your palm; you got it
rent perfume

iii.

The reason for a $100
8 cm × 8 cm change purse (for example):
"We do this shit for the cash," Maya said.
"But feel so bad about how we got it
we can't get rid of it fast enough."

iv.

Savings: LOL

v.

Being broke, then (my idea of)
not broke, an hour later
an adrenaline rush
as well as how easily
(or if not that then quickly)
I wished other life problems could be solved

vi.

The cash being the balm.
And if you did the job and got
cheated out of your balm?
Right now was when I needed something
to make me feel better
next time was too far away
(a cash loss was also a mourning)

vii.

If a guy was an asshole or stank
I'd try to charge him more
which was difficult in escort
but sometimes worked; if it did
I considered his assholery/stench paid for

viii.

The range of things I considered buyable/sellable

ix.

Men, also known as ATMs
surprise! The dehumanised will
dehumanise back (what bitches)
(oughta be dead bitches)

x.

The backroom of a takeaway chicken shop
the scuzzy couch in a night watchman's storeroom
the grimy rooming houses:
these places felt worse than high-end hotels
even if the men were not always worse

xi.

A cloud of filth, floating
a mouthful of grit and lint and you can't spit
the sense of shame, stretching, like dough
shame dough

In Dreams and in the Dead

And little low gate, with little low latch, a half nod
at the idea of keeping something out
or suggesting something in

sad as a flickering television
the patchwork path with grasses scything over

stairs tongue-crumbling
and gabled roof moon-pointing; the shriek

of the screen door
the sucked through teeth, cylinder inhale

then resistant release
as I trudge-floated through, waving to my driver
his leaf and gravel crumple-slunch then gliding away

as, "You're too tall," the man said,
looking me up and down. "And you're not eighteen
but whatever." The sigh, the world

don't get it right
here's more proof; on the stairs
dry puddles with salt-rimmed shorelines
like that other carpet, 'worn rock hard', remember
I didn't, that is
only in images that sat next to understanding

the staircase banister, tapping it
clatter of cats' claws into the night; to say

this was me feels wrong
to say this wasn't me
equally wrong; to say
I was following someone else's mind reel

with decorative swirls crafted, I imagined
for a person who had a chance once, a person

I thought not here any more. Touchable surfaces
more like a thought experiment:
if this were me, then? And arrive
at surprise, again (again)
just like a trauma, repetition not progression

the rutting of a key in a lock
the scrounge, and the
insinuate. The greenhouse hothouse belching rad
and dankness mould-charred and topsy-turvy

wading through the yellow mud air
clodded whispers and loamy intimations
of all I have witnessed of what they call

desire?

In the dead of the quiet time
I was in a steam room, I was in a brackish lagoon
muzzled in my carapace.
"You're not new either, like they said." He snorted.
"I can tell."
I shrugged. Whatever

right? Was it my arm that was yellow as well
(putting down my purse)
or the light from the bare bulb, an underwater alibi
or halo after swimming
(red-eyed from chlorine), the sheen
on his face and chartreuse bald pate

on his forehead a cut, suppurating
a leaking third eye

my aim, as I understood it:
snow peas on Steeles and precious metal
blue yellow brick road

"to get you where you need to go," remember
I did, sometimes, in dreams that sat next to disbelief
that sat next to blasé and wanting

something else I did not always mistake
for a better call or a better night

Future Poem

OK but I came out of my 'post-Vancouver haze'

(I called it); I came to my senses
and quit escort

I went back to the parlours
later I found outcall massage
this was in a hotel (mostly)
but the extras were the same as the parlours
doing that felt like nothing now

which did not explain
why I still cold nerve sweated
in summer and winter, the same, "Cold skin
warm heart, right?" They
came up with it, I didn't have to
and no more grimy rooming houses; my life

was knocking on slick shiny doors
the Hilton, the Hyatt, the Four Seasons
(etc.) knee-high boots, polished leather
I was carousel and glint, I was fairy dust
(on the outside)
I was a city at night

in the shape of a heart
ruby red with gold shimmer
a child-woman with trinkets and white coat
with faux fur trim
and in my bag, always: vodka

the striped straw a periscope accordion
stuffed back in the bottle, under the cap
and go figure, the vodka diet
first diet that ever worked!
I lost weight

now the slim woman of my former dreams
(not slim enough, of course
never slim enough
but so much better at least)—and flying

through the deserted-street night
the stacked office towers glowing green
with ceiling fields of lotus
I considered myself a knower of truths

like what was really behind those offices
and suits and pretty words men said to women
whomp-da-whomp
the seams in the road heading out

on the Gardiner, from the Westin
the Royal York, the Intercontinental
to the Marriott, Mississauga (for example)
how I loved these longer cab rides
leaning back with my bottle
watching the sepia and snow blur by
the window open a hair
wind tipping the ash off my cigarette
imagining it wing up
then dovetail into our wake

and I liked wishing the cabbie good night
and striding in the doors of the hotel
through the lobby to the elevators
the confidence I had by then

and more with the flow of the years
that no one who worked for the hotel
was going to mess with me

in at two a.m., out at three
the door people, the concierge
smiled and asked how I was
we were on the same side

customer service; bad for business
to make it difficult for male guests
to get what they wanted, and I liked

the walk along hallways
following the room numbers
until the right one
written on a cardboard chewing gum sleeve
or in the little black Moleskine notebook
(a gift from a john)
put on my game face and knock

one time, at some suburban hotel
paddy wagon in the parking lot
and on one of the beds, black-and-white photos
the size of A4 notebooks
a woman lying on kitchen parquet
one leg splayed
breasts splattered with dark grey blood.
I glanced at the photos
then at the sauntering man
who smiled at me smooth

and gathered them up like leftover snacks
I half admired this consummate covering
of an oops, as well as the senselessness of it
while I gave him a foot massage
and chatted about the weather

the photos aside, this guy
straight out of central casting for cops
with his crew cut and brown suit
no visible luggage, and shoes
lined up flush in the corner; who

I wondered, would fall into such an obvious trap?
Not like the obvious ones I'd fallen into, right

but that was back in my green and clueless days
look where I was now
how far I'd come
and really, now I loved

the adrenaline of the close call
especially if it wasn't too close
just a glancing brush like that; I was in love
with the cover of the night
and thinking about all the things I wasn't
afraid of any more, according to me

cash in the bag and big breath out
I likened those plush carpets
with their swirls and flourishes
to river veins I melted along
then re(con)figured myself

at the other end:
a place where I belonged to myself again
only more than before
I thought

and then I was floating
following the wheeling hula hoops
the meander and oxbow lakes; listen
the relief, a bliss rush

I'd done it again, also re-proven:
victory
in the sense of safety
how I could go there and ensure it
this time; here's Exhibit A
and Z

and after the downtown calls if it wasn't too cold
I'd walk home: up Yonge (for example)
at three a.m., MP3 player clipped to my waist
humming past the Eaton Centre
and the new H&M on the corner
the massage parlour near College
and the smaller one a bit further up
I'd spent some time in both of them
I walked past that past

back to my apartment on Bloor
through the lobby with abstract art
and faux antique cuirass

the concierges here too
must have known how I made my money
but were always polite
and instead of a landlord with porno, etc.,

every month I handed my rent
to a smiling woman in an office
with more abstract art
who counted the bills and wrote me a receipt
we chatted about fashion and news items
and I was a quiet, quiet drunk

with monologues playing in my head (only)
like how none of those fuckers
had ever touched me, not really.
I was threadbare, a barely there girl
in my soft, snow-white coat. And you

you want me to come in from what you
call the cold? Sure.
See how the elevator numbers piano up
to number eight
hang a left then float
over fields of blue stars

sit cross-legged on the hardwood floor
with favourite lowball glass
a smooth cube, a warm block of ice
with two-inch base, platform
like lucite heels
the clunk it made when I put it down
deep-toned and like I am really here

to count the bills
even though I knew how much I had
(usually), but to feel the matte and slippery
paper in my fingers
brown, red, and green

bend them lengthwise slightly
so they sat flat in their little stack
I had value in the world
here was the paper proof

and how that proof came in, and went back out
(so slippery), and later I couldn't understand
how I'd kept none of it
but in the meantime
floorboards and bills, with music playing
and vodka going down like easy; yes

this was what a friend was, what a home was
I thought

Epilogue

I spent ten years in the sex industry. In this book, I decided to focus on the first approximately two years of that experience, because they were the years that were most vivid in my memory, and because it was during those years I became accustomed to the industry, then entrenched in it, such that I believed prostitution was now simply my destined life.

I don't recall any light-bulb moment that prompted my decision to finally leave in 2008, although I do remember that I was severely depressed and would often stay at home and drink rather than go on calls, so I was spiralling into debt. I had visited Mexico a few years earlier and adored the culture, and I got the idea that I wanted to live there. I knew if I stayed in Toronto I'd never quit—it was too easy to go back to it as soon as my plans to do something else failed. I used the Bachelor of Arts degree I'd completed prior to arriving in Canada to apply for a job teaching English in Mexico. That education opened a path not available to the majority of women in this industry.

I made this life-changing decision while drunk. I left Canada with my suitcase and laptop, mounting credit card debt, a massive helping of unacknowledged trauma and fear, and the deep-seated belief that there was actually nothing else in the world I could do to make money.

It may come as no surprise that I was a lousy employee at the school in Mexico. It seemed that all the lack of self-worth prostitution had reinforced in me (readers of this book will know that I started off with a lot of that already in place)—had come along with me. Accordingly, I fled again. In a partial alcoholic blackout I got on a bus to the random destination of Puerto Vallarta, where I promptly met and moved in with a man from the US who beat me up on a regular basis. On some level I knew I was hoping he would do what I didn't have the 'courage' (as I saw it then) to do myself: kill me. But that story properly belongs to another book. I mention it here by way of saying that, in my case, exiting prostitution was only the beginning in terms of dealing with the damage that prostitution left behind.

However, after I made it through 2008 and 2009, slowly some things in my life started to improve. I moved out of the violent man's house into an apartment I like to describe as ultra-budget—one of the 'walls' was made of ripped plastic and bits of chicken wire, and toads the size of bocce balls hopped in when it rained. But once, a hummingbird flew in too. And my neighbour would come over to help me relocate the toads. I was making friends and finding a community—and at last, a place that felt like home.

For income, I did some Thai massage (legitimate; no extras). I'd done a certificate course in it years earlier; it had been one of those job plans that hadn't panned out in Canada. I also started writing poetry, which I loved. And I entered Alcoholics Anonymous (AA). I was unable to stay sober more than a few days at first—or stick to a tapering-off schedule for the high doses of benzodiazepines that my system was by then accustomed to—and there were to be more disastrous consequences of my drinking and pill taking. But I did 'keep coming back', as they said. And I started to glimpse some hope. I heard other people share stories about the tough periods in their lives that they had overcome. Maybe the same was possible for me?

I didn't tell many people about the life I'd left behind in Canada, because of the stigma attached to it. While men are often able to share freely about paying prostitutes (and it's often read as 'cool'), it's a much tougher undertaking for a woman to say she was a prostitute. The reactions to revealing that fact to the wrong people can feel annihilating.

I remember the day I told my AA sponsor about it. We were sitting on some large rocks in the lush jungle of Nayarit state, north of Puerto Vallarta. To one side of us was a small waterfall. Lianas twisted their tangled, light-seeking path around the oil palms and giant parota trees, and the jungle rustled and buzzed with life. I didn't want to tell her, but talking about my past life was part of my step work for AA, and I wanted to get sober. Her reaction was the opposite of what I had expected. She told me that one day I was going to be able to reach another woman who had been through similar experiences. "This history of yours is a gift," she said. Then she talked more about how my experience could benefit others.

I didn't believe her on that day or for many years afterwards. The shame, self-blame, and trauma was lodged so deeply in my being that I didn't know there was any other way for me to feel. That shifted, in the way ingrained beliefs mostly do I think: very, very slowly, and most days I couldn't see where I was going through the fog. In general though, life got better—as long as I stayed sober. And I started to get some longer stretches of sober time, until I finally took my last drink at the beginning of 2015 (I had quit the pills and other drugs earlier, sometime in 2010). My eating disorder also left me, at the same time my active alcoholism did.

Eventually, it was with my then-sponsor (and now dear friend's) words in mind that I embarked on writing this book. I hope what I've written helps someone. I also hope it shines a light on an industry that does enormous damage, overwhelmingly to women and girls, and that dehumanises everyone. I am grateful to have survived the industry and the damage it left behind, and to be able to tell my story in a public way, in the form of this book. I am one of the very lucky ones.

Notes

Book epigraph from Cathy Caruth, *Trauma: Explorations in Memory*, edited and with introductions by Cathy Caruth. The Johns Hopkins UP, 1995. p. 152. (italics hers.)

Portal, 1997

p. 6, Steeles: a major east-west street that also forms the boundary between the City of Toronto and York Region to the north.

This Gets Messed up Pretty Quickly

p. 24, the Bay: Hudson's Bay department store.

p. 25, "jizz all over your hands for ten bucks": in the parlours I experienced in Toronto at that time a half-hour massage (which was understood by seasoned punters to include a hand job) cost the man $40, out of which the house kept $30 and you kept $10. To make more than $10 you either had to expect a man to give you more money because he felt like it (not a reliable option), or negotiate for extras, which were also called 'tips'—another euphemism, as they were not actually gratuities, but rather specific prices for specific acts.

p. 30, the Leafs: The Toronto Maple Leafs, Toronto's pro ice hockey team.

Ladybugs and Wishes

p. 46, "doubles": in all the parlours I experienced, this meant one male customer with two female masseuses.

Chariot

p. 52, "who'd got stuck with a ticket": these tickets were given out by the licencing board for doing massages without a massage licence. As far as I remember this was not a criminal charge, but it involved a fine and a court appearance.

Well I Got to Vancouver and All I Found Were Brothels

p. 61, "the Grim Reaper advertisement on TV": a controversial 1987 Australian TV ad, aimed at raising HIV awareness. It featured a dystopian bowling alley in which a hooded reaper knocked people dead with bowling balls.

Red Velvet Suite

p. 68, "roofies": Rohypnol, a benzodiazepine that became known as a 'date rape' drug.

p. 76, "theft of services": a term sometimes used for the situation that occurs when a john doesn't pay. Others, including various judges, have used it instead of the word 'rape', when the woman raped is involved in the sex industry.

An Act of Glossing Over

p. 79, Words in italics are definitions of 'to gloss over' and various synonyms, taken from the Merriam-Webster online dictionary, the Cambridge online dictionary, Britannica.com, Thesaurus.com, and Wikipedia.

Home Sweet

p. 101, *Eye Weekly*: a free Toronto newspaper.

p. 102, "rads": short for radiators (heating). These were the heavy, wall-mounted types.

Mr Donut

p. 114, "loonies and toonies": one- and two-dollar coins in Canada.

To protect privacy, the names of people in this book have been changed, including fake names. Identifying details about people other than me have also been changed, and people have been combined into composite characters. Parlours and brothels are also all composites of real places.

Additionally, some important events that happened in my life during this time have been left out in order to maintain the topic focus I chose for the book, and timelines have occasionally been altered. A short amount of time between the end of Part II and the beginning of Part III has been left out, along with those events.

Acknowledgements

Thank you to Spinifex Press for publishing writing that speaks out against 'sex work' culture. My enormous gratitude to Susan Hawthorne for her interest in my project, her feedback, and her encouragement, and to Susan Hawthorne, Renate Klein, and Pauline Hopkins for their editorial attention and perceptive suggestions. It's been an immense honour and pleasure to be edited in such a comprehensive, thoughtful, and engaged way.

Thank you to the rest of the Spinifex crew: Rachael McDiarmid, Caitlin Roper, Maralann Damiano, and Sharyn Murphy. Thank you to Deb Snibson for coming up with the perfect cover, and to typesetter Helen Christie for her beautiful work.

My gratitude to the editors of the following journals, in which parts of this book have been published, in slightly or very different forms: *Bareknuckle Poet, Cordite, Overland,* and *Pink Cover Zine* (Australia); *Barrelhouse, Lana Turner, Prelude,* and *Rise Up Review* (USA); *Tinfish* (USA/Pacific); and *Event* (Canada).

Thank you to my wonderful friends Sandy Bloom Munguia, Louise Barnard, Sam Elliott, Maryse Forget, and Eileen Brewer, for their unconditional love and support, and especially as I struggled to come to terms with being open about this part of my life.

And finally, to all my fellowship friends in Puerto Vallarta, Mexico, as well as around the world. If I had never found you, I doubt I would have still been here to write any of this.

Other books by Spinifex Press

**Prostitution Narratives:
Stories of Survival in the Sex Trade**

Edited by Caroline Norma and Melinda Tankard Reist

For too long the global sex industry and its vested interests have dominated the prostitution debate repeating the same old line that sex work is just like any job. In large sections of the media, academia, public policy, Government and the law, the sex industry has had its way. Little is said of the damage, violation, suffering, and torment of prostitution on the body and the mind, nor of the deaths, suicides and murders that are routine in the sex industry.

Prostitution Narratives: Stories of Survival in the Sex Trade refutes the lies and debunks the myths spread by the industry through the lived experiences of women who have survived prostitution.

The women describe the way prostitution destroys a person's identity, health and self-worth, leaving them without safety or a rightful place in the world. The world owes a debt of gratitude to these women for their courage in speaking out against the most cruel, organized economic system in the world. These narratives should serve as a rallying cry for action to end this modern-day slave trade.
—Donna M. Hughes, Professor Chair in Women's Studies, University of Rhode Island and editor of *Dignity: A Journal of Analysis of Exploitation and Violence*

Whatever your stand on prostitution, it's the first-hand stories of women that have to be listened to first. These accounts are among the most unsettling you will ever read, dispelling in just a few pages the comforting fairytales our society has built around 'sex work'.
—Steve Biddulph, author of *Raising Boys*

ISBN 9781742199863

Not For Sale:
Feminists Resisting Prostitution and Pornography

Edited by Christine Stark and Rebecca Whisnant

This international anthology brings together research, heartbreaking personal stories from survivors of the sex industry, and theory from over thirty women and men—activists, survivors, academics and journalists. *Not For Sale* is groundbreaking in its breadth, analysis and honesty.

We've needed a current reminder that feminist resistance to systems of prostitution and pornography is still happening and resonating in audible and fervent ways. Such a need has been met with [this] anthology. *Not for Sale* offers an eclectic range of voices and writings that challenge and contest the normalization of the sex industry. *Not for Sale* is a must read for all—from longstanding radical feminists to those just coming into their feminist consciousness.
    —Garine Roubinian, *Rain and Thunder*

This three-part book is a timely and necessary addition to debates surrounding issues of prostitution and pornography. It firmly places human and civil rights at the core of the debate, and examines the connection of prostitution and pornography to racism, poverty, colonisation, globalisation and militarism ... The scope and depth of analysis is impressive, and will be a great help to those working to end sexual assault and other violence against women.
    —Lara Fergus, *Australian Centre for the Study of Sexual Assault Newsletter*

ISBN 9781876756499

Paid For:
My Journey through Prostitution

Rachael Moran

When you are fifteen years old and destitute, too unskilled to work and too young to claim unemployment benefit, your body is all you have left to sell.

Rachel Moran grew up in severe poverty and a painfully troubled family. Taken into state care at fourteen, she became homeless and was in prostitution by the age of fifteen. For the next seven years Rachel lived life as a prostituted woman, isolated, drug-addicted, alienated.

Rachel Moran's experience was one of violence, loneliness, and relentless exploitation and abuse. Her story reveals the emotional cost of selling your body night after night in order to survive – loss of innocence, loss of self-worth and a loss of connection from mainstream society that makes it all the more difficult to escape the prostitution world.

An eloquent and affecting memoir.
   —Thuy On, *The Age*

Rachel Moran has wrought out of the depravity of the 'prostitution experience' an inspirational and brilliant memoir. Courageous and tender; ultimately her story is a searing indictment of men who buy sex.
   —Kathleen Barry, author of *Female Sexual Slavery* and
     The Prostitution of Sexuality

ISBN 9781742198620

*If you would like to know more about
Spinifex Press, write to us for a free catalogue, visit our
website or email us for further information
on how to subscribe to our monthly newsletter.*

Spinifex Press
PO Box 105
Mission Beach QLD 4852
Australia

www.spinifexpress.com.au
women@spinifexpress.com.au